Advance Pra
Reimagining Customer Se

"As a family caregiver of my mom who had Alzheimer's disease, navigating the healthcare system was stressful. This book is a must-read for healthcare professionals who want to make seeking healthcare services easier for patients and their caregivers."

—**Lauren Miller Rogen**, Filmmaker and Co-Founder, HFC (formerly Hilarity for Charity)

"In *Reimagining Customer Service in Healthcare*, Jennifer puts her talents on display. Through the poignant anecdotes she shares about the past experiences that people bring with them to the healthcare encounter, particularly after damaging COVID-19 restrictions, it's easy to tell that she is both extremely discerning and laudably non-judgmental. She has a gift for empathizing with the diverse perspectives of others, and she uses that gift to effectively communicate how healthcare leaders can definitively improve the patient experience."

—**Dr. Joseph Ladapo**, Author of ***Transcend Fear: A Blueprint for Mindful Leadership in Public Health***, Professor, University of Florida College of Medicine, and Surgeon General of Florida

"*Reimagining Customer Service in Healthcare* engages in a timely conversation on the need for healthcare professionals and health systems to improve their customer service and begin to monitor the customer experience. This book provides easy to implement concepts and ideas that can make an immediate impact."

—**Michelle D. Zinnert, CAE**, Chief Executive Officer, American Urogynecologic Society

"*Reimagining Customer Service in Healthcare* is replete with personal stories which made it an easy read and easy to relate to. Jennifer FitzPatrick provides many practical examples, some of which are quite simple, to enhance customer satisfaction. If everyone read and applied the book's recommendations, the world of senior living Residents, their families, and Associates would be brighter."

—**Don Feltman**, President and CEO, Artis Senior Living

"Jennifer understands the workforce crisis that is affecting residents and caregivers. The emphasis on 'Creating a Contagious Camaraderie Culture' supports the importance of treating employees with kindness, compassion, and empathy. This culture for any business will revitalize the team so they can embrace the demands of each day and make the resident/family experience better."

—**Margie Zelenak**, Executive Director, Pennsylvania Assisted Living Association (PALA)

"Jennifer FitzPatrick's second book is not so much an owner's manual for customer service as much as a thoughtfully structured narrative on how healthcare leaders can 'do it better.' The book is an engaging read due to the illustrative examples and pop culture references to drive home the key concepts and includes timely content on the impact of the COVID-19 pandemic on everything from provider and patient experiences to Zoom fatigue. The inclusion of interviews of key leaders in the field and their best practices are valuable mirrors to our own mindsets and operating principles. This, and the inclusion of useful tools (e.g., the professional boundaries scale) make this a valuable resource for any healthcare leader—novices and experts alike."

—**Miguel Paniagua, MD**, Adjunct Professor of Medicine, Perelman School of Medicine at the University of Pennsylvania, and Vice President of Medical Education, American College of Physicians

"FitzPatrick illustrates the decline of the doctor-patient relationship since 2020 with moving personal narratives—patients and family members treated callously by those who promised to place beneficence, the well-being of the patient, first. Instead, medical professionals chose to follow unscientific government mandates and act from their own fear-driven biases, violating the very foundations of ethical medical practice. These wounds will not heal quickly. Acknowledging the damage done, however, must be the first step in repairing it. Are physicians and their staff up to the task?"

—**Mark McDonald, MD**, Author of ***United States of Fear: How America Fell Victim to a Mass Delusional Psychosis*** and ***Freedom From Fear: A 12 Step Guide to Personal and National Recovery***

"Ms. FitzPatrick's book provides sound practical advice for improving the healthcare experience for both providers and patients. Her book is especially relevant during this time of unprecedented stress for professionals and consumers. Through anecdotes and thoughtful insights, her advice is achievable and will result in a better health care experience for all."

—**Maribeth Bersani**, Gerontologist and former Chief Operating Officer, Argentum

"I am enjoying the read, disappointed every time I have to set it down, and can't wait to return to it each day! I ***really*** want everyone on our staff to read your book!"

—**Holly Ricci, DC**, Co-Founder, Annapolis Family Chiropractic

"Healthcare professionals have received substantial training to develop their medical skills, but most of the training is for specific tasks, procedures, and policies. Having empathy and communicating with patients experiencing various mental, physical, and even social feelings, emotions, and emergencies is not normally studied in depth, nor practiced in trainings. Thank you, Jennifer FitzPatrick for bringing attention to this shortcoming in healthcare and for providing practical examples and strategies for improving those experiences. The examples provided were very relatable and presented in a manner to make me think of my own experiences and interactions. The presentation style of the information provided insight into potentially traumatic experiences while inserting enough humor to keep it from being overwhelming. If you are interested in learning insights on how you may be able to improve your healthcare services in getting to know your clients better leading to better care and compliance by clients, then I recommend you read *Reimagining Customer Service in Healthcare*."

—**Judy Hackler**, Executive Director, Virginia Assisted Living Association

"Patients and clients in healthcare are not just comparing you to other hospitals or doctors' offices. They are comparing you to every other service experience they've had, and this is a tough expectation for healthcare leaders to meet. *Reimagining Customer Service in Healthcare* is your guide to exceeding those expectations while creating ***Moments of Magic*** for stressed out healthcare patients and clients."

—**Shep Hyken, CSP, CPAE**, *New York Times* Bestselling Author of ***I'll Be Back***, Chief Amazement Officer, Shepard Presentations

"This book is full of practical advice for engaging patients where they are in their healthcare journey. Mental health is such an important issue but not often provided the attention that it requires for high quality care. The book presents mental health management in an easy to understand format for all provider types."

—**Jennifer Kennedy, EdD**, Vice President, Quality and Standards, Community Health Accreditation Partner (CHAP), and Adjunct Faculty, Health Care Management, Interprofessional Health and Aging Studies, University of Indianapolis

"This book is a worthy and relaxing read. At a time in the world when kindness and customer service matter, this read offers a variety of concepts capable of replication and implementation!"

—**MaryEllen Hope Kosturko, DNP, MAHSM, RN, CENP**, Senior Vice President and Chief Nursing Officer, Yale New Haven Health/Bridgeport Hospital, CT

"Jennifer's book for healthcare leaders is a great reminder for how we as healthcare professionals need to respond to our clients. As a pharmacist, it's easy to get caught up in trying to multi-task and get the job done in an efficient manner. But her book reminded me that whatever healthcare situation the client or patient is in, they are probably not there by choice, so I need to slow down and communicate to them like I would want to be communicated with."

—**Lee Allison Boris, RPh,** Licensed Consultant Pharmacist, Express Care Pharmacy

"Jennifer uses real-life scenarios to relay her message in a way that is easy to understand, whether readers are seasoned healthcare professionals or laypeople. This book does not have to be read from cover to cover, but is a valuable guide that can be opened to any chapter in order to glean valuable information and strategies on best practices necessary to become true leaders in customer service."

—**Jenni Williams**, Director of Professional Development and Communications, National Association of Social Workers–MD Chapter

"*Reimagining Customer Service in Healthcare* is a rare glimpse into the feelings of those seeking our support: family caregivers—people who are tired, stressed, frustrated, desperate for help. To be able to put ourselves in their shoes, and to keep this perspective as we provide care and services, allows us to be mindful of how kind, patient, and professional we must be to help meet their needs as we meet the needs of their loved ones. This is the greatest gift we could provide."

—**Cole Smith, MA**, Corporate Director of Dementia Services, Brightview Senior Living

"What matters as much as great care? Great service does and Jennnifer FitzPatrick has put together an arsenal of good material in an easy-to-read format. Successful healthcare leaders understand the need to focus on superior patient experience."

—**Laurie Guest, CSP, CPAE**, Guest Enterprises, Inc.

"Jennifer FitzPatrick presents simple marketing concepts for today practitioners; a 'must-read' for healthcare professionals seeking professional insights for messaging their services now and into the future."

—**Jamey Boudreaux, MSW, MDiv**, Executive Director, Louisiana-Mississippi Hospice and Palliative Care Organization (LMHPCO)

"A thriving healthcare organization aligns its leaders' mindset with its organization's culture and values. Jennifer provides practical steps to maximize the patient experience and applies them to multiple healthcare sectors. Her insight is spot on and packaged for success. This book is a must-read for healthcare leaders committed to driving care excellence, employee engagement, and customer satisfaction."

—**Jerald Cosey**, Operational Leadership Development Director, American Senior Communities

"'How does one make everyone happy?' That's what went through my mind when I first began a management role that required thoughtful leadership. I quickly learned, while I cannot satisfy everyone, I can, very artfully, make sure that everyone feels valued and heard. The approach to customer service within the healthcare realm is multifaceted because your audience is vast and includes team members, patients/residents, families, state surveyors, vendors, etc. Jennifer's book does an exemplary job of explaining how one can level up their customer service skills. It's an easy and engaging read for all."

—**Shilpa Patel**, Regional Director of Operations, Merrill Gardens

"*Reimagining Customer Service in Healthcare* is a love letter to the ideals and actions that truly deliver outstanding patient care experiences. Add this book to your shelf. It dives into the compassion and attention to detail it takes to achieve service excellence in all care environments."

—**Joe Mull, MEd, CSP**, Author of *Cure for the Common Leader: What Physicians & Managers Must Do to Engage & Inspire Healthcare Teams*

"Clients enter the healthcare system with a variety of presenting issues and diverse personal backgrounds, further complicated by a global pandemic. Using engaging vignettes and real life examples while capitalizing on her background in psychotherapy, FitzPatrick clearly illustrates best practices for customer service across healthcare industries as well as places where organizations and individuals may fall short. With her approachable writing style, she lays out a roadmap to guide healthcare leaders as they create a positive environment where employees feel valued and clients leave their interactions feeling grateful, not hateful. I highly recommend that anyone in a leadership position or with aspirations of leadership in healthcare read this book. It quickly reminds us why we pursue careers in health, and the difference we can make with both small gestures and larger systemic changes."

—**Kelly Fiala, PhD**, Dean, College of Health and Human Services at Salisbury University

"This is the best healthcare related book I've ever read. Filled with practical and proven strategies, this book is a must-read for healthcare providers seeking a competitive edge. ***Reimagining Customer Service in Healthcare*** is a thoroughly engaging and compelling read, filled with relatable real-life examples that hit home on both a professional and personal level. FitzPatrick expertly illustrates how understanding and applying the customers' point of view is a win-win, resulting in optimal outcomes for all stakeholders."

—**Rebekah Goetz**, **MSM**, Vice President, Montcordia

"Reimagining Customer Service in Healthcare is a how-to book on providing great customer service. Through real life examples, Jennifer illustrates simple tips that can change a customer from 'hateful' to 'grateful.' Her focus on building and living a strong culture, the importance of hiring and maintaining a workforce that believes in the culture, and understanding who and where your customers are in their unique journey, provides a roadmap to improved customer service. This is an easy read that will leave you eager to develop a 'Contagious Camaraderie Culture.'"

—**Nicole Bartecki,** Vice President of Sales and Marketing, Anthem Memory Care

REIMAGINING CUSTOMER SERVICE *in Healthcare*

Boost Loyalty, Profits, and Outcomes

JENNIFER L. FITZPATRICK, MSW, CSP

A POST HILL PRESS BOOK
ISBN: 978-1-63758-682-2
ISBN (eBook): 978-1-63758-683-9

Reimagining Customer Service in Healthcare:
Boost Loyalty, Profits, and Outcomes

Cover design by Tiffani Shea

Interior Design by Yoni Limor, www.yonilimor.com

Post Hill Press
New York • Nashville
posthillpress.com

Published in the United States of America
1 2 3 4 5 6 7 8 9 10

This book is dedicated to the memory of my Dad, Hank Lubaczewski. Hank was a one-of-a-kind character, and I'm sure he was regarded by some health and mental health providers as an "Always Difficult" Patient. He was also a lot of fun, and the most generous and least judgmental person I've ever known. He is missed, loved, and remembered daily by his kids, sisters, and family.

CONTENTS

PART THREE

Transforming Their Mindset and Experience

INTRODUCTION

Your patients and clients hate that they need you. There's no way around that fact. They wish they didn't have a problem that they need you to help them solve. This is universally true for all areas of healthcare, mental healthcare, senior living, and any ancillary medical or health-related service. No patient or client is excited to call your office, turn on their computer for a telehealth appointment, or walk through your doors.

Even if your organization is at the top of its game, your patients, clients, and their family caregivers *still* wish they didn't need you. Even if you have wait lists. Even if you are the "preferred provider" in your area. As Dr. Thomas Lee says in his book *An Epidemic of Empathy in Healthcare: How to Deliver Compassionate, Connected Patient Care That Creates a Competitive Advantage*,[1] "No institution can rest on its laurels because it has a fabulous reputation."

If you work in any of the aforementioned practice settings, this book will help you transform reluctant customers—your clients, patients, and family caregivers—from feeling "hateful" to feeling "grateful." How? This book is filled with ideas (some big, but most small; some expensive, but most economical or free) on how to improve the experience your clientele has when they interact with you.

Most people drawn to this book already embrace the link between engaging your patient or client and achieving better clinical outcomes. But there are still healthcare leaders and clinicians who believe that their focus should strictly be on clinical outcomes. As a healthcare speaker, I have encountered a lot of professionals who don't believe there's value in trying to improve customer service, bedside manner, patient engagement strategies, or whatever their organization is calling it. Let's just focus on getting people better, they say.

If you are one of the skeptics who feels this way, I get it! After all, you studied to become a licensed professional: a doctor, a psychologist, a physical therapist, a nurse. You went to medical school or nursing school, not charm school! You didn't major in business, and you don't care about online reviews or whether or not the patient likes you. You care about curing that child with osteosarcoma. Your goal is to get that patient with depression to feel incrementally better. You want that resident who has dementia to have better quality of life.

I respect your point of view. But I am asking if you will consider reading this book with an open mind. Can you be open to the possibility that embracing strategies that transform patients and clients from hating that they need you to being glad they met you will make your job and the lives of those you serve easier? In addition to my own experiences and observations, I will share the literature along with specific patient-experience advice from my personal interviews with more than twenty healthcare leaders and executives including:

- Dr. Allan Anderson (Banner Health)
- Daniel Blum (Sinai Hospital of Baltimore; LifeBridge Health)
- Chad Brough (Home Instead Senior Care)
- Terri Cunliffe (Covenant Living Communities and Services)

- John Dumas (Service Coordination Inc.)
- Dr. Naim El-Aswad (Vital Signs Vital Skills LLC; Warrior Recovery Center)
- Rick Evans (NewYork-Presbyterian Hospital)
- Dr. Kathryn Fiddler (TidalHealth)
- Peggy Funk, (Hospice & Palliative Care Network of Maryland)
- Heather Guerieri, (Compass)
- Jeff Frum (Silverado)
- Kevin Goedeke (Erickson Senior Living; NHA Stand-Up LLC)
- Anton Gunn (formerly of Medical University of South Carolina)
- Dr. Arif Kamal (American Cancer Society; Duke University)
- George King (For All Seasons Inc.)
- James Lee (Bella Groves)
- Dr. Alan Levin (NewYork-Presbyterian Queens Hospital)
- Denise Manifold (Brightview Senior Living)
- Janice Martin (Senior Liaison of Central Florida Inc.)
- Leslie Ray (LCB Senior Living)
- Cara Silletto (Magnet Culture)

While C-suite executives and leaders are quoted throughout *Reimagining Customer Service in Healthcare*, this book was written not just for leaders but for individuals serving in clinical or support staff roles as well. Although I've been CEO of Jenerations Health Education for well over a decade, I have a long history of trying to improve customer service in a variety of roles that some of you not yet in the C-suite might relate to. Early in my career, I answered phones and made copies as a receptionist in a nursing home. I wiped butts at an adult day care center. I have managed and marketed healthcare programs at for-profit and government organizations. I have counseled individuals, couples, and families as a psychotherapist. With that background as both a leader and a worker bee, and with the viewpoint of a former shrink, I am going to help you better understand the mindset of your patients and clients so you can help them *get better* while they *feel better* about working with you. Let's begin!

Author's Note: The vignettes and case examples used throughout the book are comprised of composite characters.

PART ONE

Inside the Mindset of Your Clients, Patients, and Their Family Caregivers

Part One explores the mindset and attitudes your patients, clients, and their family caregivers present when you begin to work with them. In this section, we are going to dive into how your customers think about you and why some of them can be particularly challenging to serve.

CHAPTER 1
Are They All Really "Hateful"?

Do you look forward to needing a healthcare service for yourself or a loved one? Most people would say no. But you are not most people. You work in healthcare and are far more familiar with navigating "the system" than the vast majority. You have the distinct advantage of knowing what to expect when procuring healthcare services, what your options are, and whom to speak with when there's a problem. But I bet your answer to the above question is still also a big fat "no." Needing a doctor, hospital, or other healthcare service is never fun! It's certainly not like buying a new pair of shoes or splurging on a nice vacation or dinner.

Consider the last time you, a healthcare professional, needed some service on the healthcare continuum. Despite knowing what to expect and how to advocate, you probably weren't excited about it. Even if the service you needed was routine and nonthreatening, like your annual physical, it's still not something to look forward to. But what about when the stakes are higher—when you need a rehab center for your teenage son who overdosed? Or when your sister has been in a serious car accident? Clearly, most people aren't in a happy, calm state of mind when they discover they need healthcare services. Simply put, your patients, clients, and their family members are SOA (stressed on arrival).

I have been working in healthcare since I was sixteen. So even though I know how to advocate from within and navigate our complex system, I dread it just like you. Here are just a few of my unpleasant experiences:

- feeling weight-shamed by my primary care physician when my weight climbed to an embarrassingly high number

- navigating the mental health system for my very high-functioning, cognitively intact father when he was chronically and alternatively suicidal and homicidal for over twenty years

- visiting senior living communities to determine the best fit for my grandmother, whom our family could no longer take care of at home

I'm sure you have plenty of personal examples too!

The feelings associated with accessing healthcare services are typically quite negative; patients generally don't feel as though "it's about them." In fact, many of them enter your organization feeling downright "hateful."

While not every client or patient entering the healthcare system should be described as "hateful," it's safe to say they wish they didn't need you. Patients dreading an annual routine physical are likely significantly less "hateful" than patients moving into a nursing home. But the typical patient coming in for the physical exam still does not enjoy making time in her busy schedule to drive to your office, answer personal or intrusive questions, and take off her clothes. Most people clearly *dislike* the idea of needing surgery, assisted living, home care, mental health counseling, physical therapy, or any other service on the healthcare spectrum for themselves or a loved one, even those services considered mundane.

In fact, there are actually specific phobias associated with our industry that plague many of our patients and clients. Let's look at a few:

- Iatrophobia (fear of doctors, medical tests)
- Tomophobia (excessive anxiety when thinking about upcoming surgeries or other healthcare procedures)
- Nosocomephobia (an extreme fear of hospitals)
- Hemophobia (fear of blood)
- Trypanophobia (fear of needles)

Many people who experience these phobias will describe panic symptoms and even panic attacks at simply the *idea* of engaging with you. For some people, driving by a hospital or the thought of getting blood drawn causes anxiety symptoms such as racing heart rate, breathlessness, stomach upset, light-headedness, trembling, chills, and sweating.

This can be really hard to imagine for those of you who aren't mental health specialists. Let me explain it this way: Have you ever watched a really suspenseful movie? The 2012 movie *Argo* is one. The film is about how CIA agent Tony Mendez, played by Ben Affleck, gets American hostages out of Iran. A true story, everyone in the movie theater knew how it would end. Despite that, I found myself holding my breath and tensing up as the plane with the hostages lifted off Iranian soil. My husband, Sean, nudged me and jokingly whispered, "You know they get out, right?" It didn't matter that I already knew they got out. I was so engrossed in the story that my body had a physical response.

People with healthcare-specific phobias have bought into the story that something bad is going to happen to them when they engage with you and your organization. While iatrophobia, tomophobia, nosocomephobia, hemophobia, and trypanophobia are true anxiety disorders, patients are not wrong to have some reservations about interacting with the health and mental health system. Not only is there a chance that we will give patients bad news when they engage with us, we are also decidedly imperfect.

It's widely reported that at least 250,000 Americans die every year because of healthcare mistakes. In fact, some studies suggest that medical errors are the third leading cause of death in the United States.[2] Bad news about healthcare is also widely reported by the media, which doesn't endear us to the public. When a celebrity is involved, there's even more press. Consider the case of actor Dennis Quaid's newborn baby twins who nearly died from a major medication error. Comedienne Joan Rivers's death was covered by the media as a routine procedure gone wrong. What about the death of pop star Michael Jackson, whose doctor was allegedly putting him to sleep with the anesthetic propofol?

But even stories of "regular people" featured in the media stress out our patients and clients. Sorrel King's inspiring book, *Josie's Story*,[3] details the unthinkable, accidental death of her eighteen-month-old daughter, Josie, at none other than Johns Hopkins Hospital. This child, who was on the mend from a second-degree burn, died of dehydration under the watch of healthcare providers at one of the most famous medical centers in the world. (More on Sorrel King's incredible story later.) It's no wonder that patients and clients hate the thought of walking through our doors after having heard these news stories. Never mind the rants about bad healthcare experiences they hear from friends, neighbors, and, maybe even more importantly, on social media.

Let's not forget the large number of clients and patients who have had bad experiences with the health and mental healthcare systems because of their minority status. It's hard to overstate the hesitancy many Black individuals feel about the healthcare system because of the Tuskegee Study. What about LGBTQ+ persons who were told that they were mentally ill because of their sexual orientation? (It was only in 1973 that the American Psychological Association reversed its position that being gay was a mental health condition.) Still others have experienced discrimination because of their religious beliefs and socioeconomic statuses. Even if an individual did not directly experience discrimination, distrust and dislike of the health and mental health system, concerns are frequently passed down from generation to generation by those who have.

Even if you wouldn't describe all your patients or clients as "hateful," you certainly have observed their negative feelings about needing you. That's not to say that many patients don't ultimately come to like and trust their providers. A woman struggling with infertility may think her reproductive endocrinologist does a wonderful job. Three daughters who were struggling caring for their mom and were reluctant to outsource her care may eventually appreciate their mother's home care provider. But most people simply don't start out eager to need or search for those services.

In *Service Fanatics*,[4] Dr. James Merlino, chief experience officer of the Cleveland Clinic, states, "Patients don't just need our services. They come to us at their most vulnerable and often at the most frightening time of their lives, and they put those lives in our hands." Let's explore some of the feelings your patients experience when they surrender themselves to the healthcare system.

- **Self-blame.** *Why didn't I take better care of myself?* Sitting in the waiting room of an oncologist's office, seventy-three-year-old Rose beats herself up. She thinks back to first time she took a drag of a cigarette sixty years prior with her eighth-grade boyfriend in the park behind their parochial school in Chicago. Worried about what the oncologist will say, she thinks, *I can't believe I'm here.... Why didn't I listen to all the doctors.... I'm so stupid.*

- **Nervousness**. Fifty-year-old David is completing the pre-op paperwork for his kidney transplant surgery. While he knows the surgery is necessary, he thinks of his wife, Lucy, and their two young sons. His heart pounds, and his thoughts dart around like a pinball machine: *What if I die during this procedure and leave my family behind? Could Lucy really handle the kids and the house on her own. I probably should've purchased more life insurance when I was eligible—what if it's not enough? What if there's a medical mistake? What if I can't go back to work? What if I wake up during surgery and can't communicate? What if the kidney they give me doesn't work like it should? What if I have to do this all over again with another donor kidney? Would they even be able to find another match?*

- **Confusion**. Twenty-eight-year-old Danielle can't figure out why she has been feeling so down in the dumps since her beautiful daughter was born two months ago. All she's ever wanted in life was to be a mom, and now her dream has come true. Because of her relentless crying, Danielle's husband and mother-in-law keep pleading with her to talk to her doctor. She's confused about her feelings and doesn't know how to articulate them to anyone, especially not her doctor, who has such limited hours. She can't figure out why she feels so bad when she's been so lucky.

- **Frustration**. Thirty-eight-year-old Janine, a real estate agent, rushes into the emergency department of a hospital more than forty miles from her home. Janine's seventy-five-year-old mother was brought via ambulance earlier because of a fall. Janine is exasperated because this is the third time her mother has fallen in the past six weeks. She is going to be late for the closing on a client's new home, and she's feeling at the end of her rope about her mom. Her thoughts of frustration are on a loop: *If my mother had moved to a one-floor apartment like I asked her to, she wouldn't have fallen! If she had worn a Life Alert pendant she wouldn't have been lying on the floor for so long. She just doesn't listen, and I don't know what will get through to her.* Janine is also frustrated because her siblings live out of state and are pretty much useless when her mother has such emergencies.

- **Embarrassment**. Nineteen-year-old Erica is a college student who knows that vomiting after meals and exercising up to six hours per day is not "normal." She thinks about talking to a doctor or psychotherapist but is too embarrassed to admit out loud that she might have a problem. What if they tell her parents? Erica's parents have such high regard for her. She would be mortified if they knew what she was doing—not to mention how humiliating it would be if her boyfriend found out.

- **Hopelessness**. Thirty-year-old Dennis has dealt with chronic headaches for three years. Although countless tests and medications have been prescribed, not one specialist has been able to help him. Even though he feels miserable all day every day, he has lost hope that anyone will be able to properly diagnose and treat him. What's the point in seeing another doctor?

- **Tension**. Thirty-five-year-old Joel suffers with obsessive-compulsive disorder. Although he takes medication for the condition, Joel struggles terribly when dealing with uncertainty. Just waiting for the results from his annual routine blood work causes him muscle tension, lost sleep, and rumination. Ironically, Joel is in excellent health, and his blood work has always been normal. Joel knows that his excessive worrying is probably irrational, but he can't seem to control his tension.

- **Fear**. Sixteen-year-old Dana is pacing in the emergency department waiting room. She was driving herself and her best friend, Olivia, back from the movies when another driver ran a red light and hit their vehicle. Olivia was unconscious when she was taken to the hospital for examination. Dana is terrified that Olivia will die or be permanently injured, and it will be all her fault. How will Olivia's belligerent parents react when they call her back and hear the news?

- **Guilt**. For the past five years, sixty-eight-year-old Catherine has been taking care of her eighty-

> two-year-old husband, Jeff, who has Parkinson's disease. After talking extensively with her caregiver support group about her burnout, she has finally decided she needs to bring some help into their home so she can take some occasional weekends away. When she tells her brother about interviewing home care agencies, he says he can't believe she would consider leaving Jeff with strangers. Is her brother right? Is she being selfish?

While none of the above individuals are outwardly "hateful," they are clearly not happy to be engaging with the healthcare system. Frequently, they are even less pleased when they have to disrupt their schedules and lives to use your services as described in Janine's case. I'm sure you could provide countless examples of other patients dealing with other unpleasant feelings.

But then again, there really are patients and clients you serve whom you *would* describe as hateful. Let's take a look at some examples:

Victor was referred to your dermatology office two weeks ago by his primary care doctor. He is on the waiting list to see a dermatologist. He calls every day, asking about the status of his appointment. Your office manager reminds him that he is on the wait list and will be called as soon as an opening becomes available. She also has offered him referrals to several other dermatology practices. He has begun writing nasty comments on your clinic's social media sites and negative reviews on websites like Healthgrades.com. Victor also has threatened to report your clinic to state regulators if he doesn't get his appointment soon.

Jason is a pharmacist working at the drive-through when Mrs. Rowe pulls up to the window to pick up three prescriptions. Mrs. Rowe becomes irate when she hears the price of one of her newly prescribed medications. She tears up and begins cursing about the state of healthcare and the inadequate coverage her insurance company provides. She asks Jason what she is supposed to do since she can't afford it, but her doctor has told her this medication is essential. Jason has heard this sort of rant from at least two other people today. He wants to show empathy, but there are a half dozen cars waiting behind Mrs. Rowe.

Dr. Martin is a dentist in private practice. Her entire staff is grumbling that Mrs. Smith is scheduled today. They all absolutely dread the days Mrs. Smith comes to the dental studio. Mrs. Smith arrives early for every single appointment and then complains that she has to wait. She hovers over the receptionist's desk even though the receptionist repeatedly invites her to take a seat. One dental hygienist has flat-out refused to treat Mrs. Smith because she has repeatedly made insulting remarks about her appearance. Mrs. Smith always insists on seeing Dr. Martin privately after every appointment to criticize everything from the staff to her bill.

Thirty-year-old Rhonda has bipolar disorder and has not been taking her medication. She has been shopping excessively and not sleeping. As a psychiatrist in a large mental health clinic, you know that psychiatric patients frequently go off their prescriptions. In a joint meeting with Rhonda and her wife, you explain why it's important for Rhonda to keep taking the medication and how her manic symptoms will likely diminish when she does. Rhonda's wife screams at you, saying that *you* have to do something now because they can't afford for Rhonda to be spending all this money. These types of outbursts are regular occurrences during your joint appointments with the couple.

Daniel's wife, Helen, has mid-stage Alzheimer's disease and has been admitted to the hospital with a urinary tract infection and dehydration. Because of COVID-19 policies, Daniel is not permitted to visit his wife. They have been married for forty-two years and are not accustomed to being apart, particularly since her diagnosis three years ago. Daniel has frantically called any and every department of the hospital he can think of, pleading his case to be by Helen's side. He explains how confused she becomes in unfamiliar places and that she sometimes doesn't even remember her own name. Daniel states that he has been vaccinated and has tested negative for COVID-19, but he is told once again that "hospital policy" prohibits visitors. Daniel responds, "You will be hearing from my attorney."

I'm guessing you have found yourself dealing with one or more of these examples at work. If you've dealt with a similar situation in your *personal* life, you probably found yourself empathizing with a few of the patients in the above scenarios.

"I once heard it said that patients are a lot like prisoners," says Dr. James Merlino in *Service Fanatics*. This comparison does not feel like an exaggeration to many patients. While those of us who work in healthcare know that we often have choices and options, most patients and their families perceive a major loss of control when they enter the healthcare system. In addition to feeling angry, guilty, scared, nervous, shame, embarrassment, and other challenging emotions, they are acutely aware of their vulnerability. Sadly, these difficult feelings patients experience are not usually de-escalated by providers as "research shows that physicians respond to only one in ten opportunities to express empathy," according to *Communication the Cleveland Clinic Way: How to Drive a Relationship-Centered Strategy for Superior Customer Service* by Dr. Adrienne Boissy and Dr. Tim Gilligan.[5]

The great news? You *can* reduce the stress of our patients and clients and improve that pitiful statistic! Even the nicest and most reasonable clients and patients are going to have difficult feelings when they begin their journey with you. While this book is going to offer lots of simple solutions on how to reduce "hateful" feelings in all your clients and patients, it's important to be able to recognize those who are less reasonable and will be particularly difficult no matter what.

Let's start the crash course: identifying and managing those with "Always Difficult" characteristics—in particular, clients and patients with personality disorder traits.

CHAPTER 2
Recognizing Whom You Are Dealing With

We've already established that nobody wants to need your services. Thankfully, most patients and clients you encounter are rooting for you and hope you get it right. They want all to go well. Once they ultimately agree to have that surgery on the knee that's been bugging them for years, they try to cooperate with discharge plans so they will feel better. Once their child gets over the initial fear of allergy shots, they eagerly anticipate fewer allergic reactions and trips to the emergency department. Upon taking the step to seek marriage counseling, they are hoping you will give them the tools to reconnect as a couple.

These patients and clients are what I call the "Usually Reasonable" people. They represent the majority of people you serve. While they aren't happy that they need you, and there can certainly be service hiccups along the way that need to be addressed, they are extremely malleable. Creating a "Contagious Camaraderie Culture," which we will discuss in chapter 7, has a huge impact on these reasonable folks. Embracing the strategies and principles of a Contagious Camaraderie Culture is the key to reducing and eliminating even mild "hateful" feelings while converting them to "grateful" ones.

But of course, you already know not everyone is like that. Not by a long shot. There are patients and clients who will be endlessly needy and unsatisfied. In fact, often it seems like some patients and clients are just waiting for you and your organization to screw up. While this is a small percentage of the population, it sometimes *feels* like they are everywhere. This is because of the time and energy you and your team spend trying to manage them. This chapter focuses on helping you recognize traits of the "Always Difficult."

Why are some people "Always Difficult"? I believe there are usually two reasons: well-known mental health conditions and the lesser-understood personality disorders. In this chapter, regardless of your background or experience with mental health, we will examine ways to identify some of these conditions. Spotting these traits will help you apply strategies (discussed in Part Three) to help improve your interactions with these clients and patients to enhance services.

Even if you don't specialize in working with psychiatric conditions, you definitely are serving (or at some point have served) patients and clients with the following diagnoses:

- Schizophrenia
- Bipolar disorder
- Anxiety disorders (including the medical-related phobias discussed in the first chapter)
- Obsessive-compulsive disorder
- Depression
- Substance use disorder

You may know people in your personal life who struggle with one or more of these conditions. It's only logical that these conditions also exist with the patients and clients you serve, even when it's not their presenting problem.

Let's examine some examples:

Lou is the chief medical officer at a major hospital. Between himself and his chief of surgery, they have received seventeen emails over the last two days from Mindy, who recently had emergency gallbladder surgery. While the surgery was successful, Mindy wants to review with them all the ways her surgical team could have better disinfected the operating room. Mindy's emails express concern that she will suffer an infection because she does not believe the room was sterile enough. Any ideas what might be going on with Mindy?

If you guessed that Mindy seems to have obsessive-compulsive disorder traits, you would be correct.

Kim is the daughter of a resident at the senior living community where Jackie is the executive director. Kim attends family care plan meetings but rarely seems to remember the details that are discussed with the team about her mother's care. Kim leaves messages for you and your team late at night at least a few times per month. The content of the messages is all over the place. Sometimes Kim compliments them; other times she complains. The one consistency about the messages is that Kim is slurring her words. Any idea what's going on with Kim?

If you guessed that Kim likely has a substance abuse problem, you'd be correct.

Steve is a chiropractor working with Tim, who has bipolar disorder. Steve treats Tim for his chronic neck and back pain, not his bipolar disorder. But every so often, when Tim goes off his medication, Steve's staff deal with a barrage of paranoid, delusional phone calls. Tim accuses them of everything from cancelling his appointments without permission to breaking into his house. Clearly, when Tim is not on his medication, he is "Always Difficult."

It's not necessary or appropriate for Lou, Jackie, or Steve to diagnose the above mental health conditions. But being *aware* of what's driving the "Always Difficult" behavior of their patients and clients will help them provide better service and outcomes.

Personality disorders—for most people except psychotherapists—tend to be more elusive and less well-known. Once I began to appreciate these conditions, my understanding of what makes people tick snapped into focus like never before. The ability to recognize personality disorder traits in both my personal and professional life has been a major game changer. It has saved me thousands of hours of wondering, *Why is this person behaving this way?*

Now that I recognize personality disorder traits in individuals, I am able to help others do the same, both professionally and personally. During countless coaching and consulting sessions with both executives and clinicians, I have watched as the light goes on. The person I am coaching will be venting about a difficult patient, client, subordinate, or colleague, seeking ways to improve communication with that person. When I gently suggest that some of their behaviors resemble narcissism, for example, it completely transforms the way the person I am coaching looks at how to approach working with that problem patient, client, or employee. My goal is to help you recognize these traits so your organization can transform these individuals from "hateful" to "grateful."

Note I said, "recognize personality disorder traits" and not "diagnose personality disorders." Unless you or I are working in the official capacity of a person's health or mental health provider, it's inappropriate for us to diagnose an individual. Back when I was a psychotherapist, I certainly diagnosed clients and patients with personality disorders as well as other mental health conditions. But because I am not currently working in a clinical capacity, I simply recognize these traits when I observe them. I can then adjust my approach to working with that individual. That's what I want to urge you and your team to try to do as well. You can then apply the skills discussed in Part Three to influence these folks.

Let's take a look at what the term "personality disorder" actually means. According to the *Diagnostic and Statistical Manual of*

Mental Disorders (DSM-5)—the mental health bible—a personality disorder is an "enduring pattern of inner experience and behavior that deviates markedly from the expectations of the individual's culture, is pervasive and inflexible, has an onset in adolescence or early adulthood, is stable over time, and leads to distress and impairment." According to the National Institute of Mental Health, 9 percent of us meet the criteria for a personality disorder. That means that nearly *thirty million Americans* meet the criteria for one or more of the ten personality disorders described in the DSM-5.

In my opinion, seven of these conditions tend to be most associated with "Always Difficult" behavior:

- Borderline personality disorder
- Narcissistic personality disorder
- Histrionic personality disorder
- Antisocial personality disorder
- Paranoid personality disorder
- Dependent personality disorder
- Obsessive compulsive personality disorder

Let's consider each one more closely.

BORDERLINE PERSONALITY DISORDER

Based on the DSM-5, here are the traits most associated with borderline personality disorder:

- Adult temper tantrums
- They either love you or hate you (and often vacillate between the two extreme emotions)

- Afraid of abandonment
- Struggles with self-image
- Engages in destructive behaviors such as acting out sexually, substance abuse, reckless driving, or gambling. (This can often make many health and mental health professionals think of bipolar disorder).
- Suicidal threats and gesturing and/or other self-harm behaviors
- Intense mood swings
- Feeling "empty"
- Tendency to fixate on paranoid ideas
- Potential to dissociate

I am going to share with you a personal example of an individual with borderline personality disorder. It was someone I knew quite well—my dad.

My father, Hank, struggled with mental health problems over the course of his entire life. Although he was a very high-functioning individual, he was no stranger to psychiatric hospitals and all sorts of other mental health treatments. Over the course of his life, he was diagnosed with many mental health conditions: bipolar disorder, major depression, substance use disorder, generalized anxiety disorder, Asperger's syndrome, and many more. To my knowledge, he was never officially diagnosed with a personality disorder. But I am absolutely convinced that borderline personality disorder was his primary issue.

Hank pretty much met all the criteria for this diagnosis. Perhaps a psychiatrist or psychotherapist at one point did diagnose him with borderline personality disorder, but it was never disclosed to our family (or to my dad). After all, many mental health professionals are reluctant to share personality disorder diagnoses with their patients and clients (for a variety of reasons). Here's why I believe borderline personality disorder was my father's primary problem:

- There was constant talk of suicide and frequent suicidal ideation. From my teenage years, I was prepared to someday get a phone call that my dad had finally taken his own life. When Hank died suddenly at age sixty-five, it took a lot of convincing for me to accept that he'd died of natural causes.

- As for reckless and impulsive behaviors...

    - Gambling: check.
    - Speeding in his Camaro: check.
    - Abusing prescription drugs and alcohol: check.
    - Sex with prostitutes: check.
    - His countless temper tantrums.

While there are too many incidents to describe, my husband, Sean, will never forget the Sunday afternoon we, Hank, and several other family members were at a tuxedo shop. We were reviewing the selection for the guys' tuxedos for our upcoming wedding. When we inquired about a "special" we'd heard advertised where the groom would get his tuxedo free with a rental of six or more suits, the clerk responded that the deal was no longer being offered. My husband and I were a bit bummed that we missed the deadline, but not overly concerned; Sean could certainly afford to rent his own tuxedo! Hank, on the other hand, became furious. He began shouting at the clerk and gathering up piles of dress shirts into his arms. He screamed that if the special was not honored, he would steal the merchandise as compensation. It took four family members to calm him down. After a few minutes of apologizing to the shop clerk, we escorted my dad out of the store.

This reaction was from a man who earned a healthy six-figure salary. His response was not about a discount or money at all. It was all about my dad's perception that we were being disrespected.

Familiarizing yourself with some of the traits of borderline personality disorder can help you identify red flags that signal this condition in your workplace. Here are some examples:

- A patient tells you what a great eye doctor you are. Several months later, he writes scathing reviews on your practice's Facebook page.

- During a routine gynecological exam, your patient brags about all the risky behavior she gets away with, like having sex without condoms.

- Patient informs your staff that she will kill herself if you don't call back within a certain period of time even though you are on maternity leave.

NARCISSISTIC PERSONALITY DISORDER

Based on the DSM-5, here are the traits most associated with narcissistic personality disorder:

- Views self as superior to others
- Struggles empathizing with others
- Egotistical behavior
- Securing admiration of others is a priority
- Feels they deserve more or better than other people
- Grandiosity
- Believes others are jealous of them
- Feels envious of other people

Here's a case study of someone I worked with who had narcissistic personality disorder traits.

Tate is a seventy-nine-year-old senior living resident. He insists that he is a VIP because his son is a well-known doctor in another state. He often boasts about how much he knows about medical issues and that he can evaluate how well the staff is treating him clinically. He talks about how special his medical issues are and that he deserves more time than other residents. When his ex-wife died, he did not offer his adult children condolences about their mother's passing. Instead, he complained that they would not be able to take him to a concert he'd been looking forward to because they'd be at the funeral. Tate often claims to the ombudsman that staff members are neglecting him. He has reported the community to the state several times, and the community has had a surprise inspection because of this. The ombudsman and state inspectors found no evidence of neglect by the senior living community. Family members of some other residents notice that Tate often gets significantly more attention than other residents and are considering moving their loved ones. Two excellent staff members have recently resigned because of Tate.

What are some of the red flags you saw in Tate's behavior?

Here are some additional indicators you might see that signal narcissistic personality disorder in your workplace:

- A client asks you regularly to meet with him outside of your normal appointment times without regard for your schedule

- Your patient demands to be moved up on the wait-list for an organ transplant because of the prestige and importance of his job

- Upon seeing your diploma hanging on the wall of your office, your client comments that she went to a more prestigious university

Some clients, patients, and family members may appear on the surface to fall into the "Always Difficult" category, but they are not. Let me tell you about Al.

When it got to the point that Al's dad could no longer take care of himself, it was incredibly stressful for their family. It got to the point where Al's father was not comfortable spending the night alone, so he and his siblings took turns sleeping over at his apartment. Eventually, they brought in-home care to augment the family's help. Ultimately, the decision was made that Al would go to senior living. As luck would have it, the community they selected had a waiting list. The staff at the community told Al's sister Nina (who was a nurse) that she was welcome to check in every couple of days to see if there had been any movement on the list.

After approximately two weeks had gone by with polite check-ins, they were no closer to securing a room at the desired community. Each time Nina got this disappointing news, she would text the family to update them. One day after receiving the text update, Al picked up the phone and said, "Nina, what do you think about calling them back and explaining the situation?" Nina asked him what he meant, he said, "Well, explain that we are paying a lot for in-home care and that we are all exhausted. That we'd really love it if they would move us up on this list." Nina, who had much experience with these sorts of situations because of her nursing background said, "Don't you think that's the same story every other family member has?" Immediately Al understood, and they had a bit of a laugh about it.

But what if Al had been the one who called the community and said that to a staff member? The person on the other end of the phone may have thought, *Wow, this is very entitled and narcissistic behavior*. But here is the difference: a "Usually Reasonable" person is typically going to have a fair reaction to your rational response. Someone who truly has narcissistic traits, probably would have pushed back and maybe would have exploded that their request was not being honored.

Oh, and just for the record, Al is one of the least narcissistic persons—and also one of the most selfless—I have ever met.

HISTRIONIC PERSONALITY DISORDER

Based on the DSM-5, here are the traits most associated with histrionic personality disorder:

- Craves being the center of attention
- Frequently sexually inappropriate, flirtatious, and/or provocative
- Dramatic behavior
- Extremely focused on appearances
- Believes relationships are "deeper" or more "serious" than the other parties
- Very impressionable

Here's a case study of someone I know who had histrionic personality disorder traits.

Carrie is a nineteen-year-old nursing student. While she regularly participates in our class discussions, her contributions typically deviate from the topic at hand. She has burst into tears during several of our class sessions. Carrie dresses in designer clothing and wears excessive makeup, always "name-dropping" the brands she dons when interacting with her classmates. She has asked me, her college instructor, whom she has only known for seven weeks, to attend a family wedding as her guest.

What red flags do you see with Carrie's behavior?

The following are examples of additional red flags you may encounter that signal possible histrionic personality disorder.

- Patient brings up healthcare theories or experts you are unfamiliar with. When you ask them to tell you more, they express disdain and disappointment that you are "ignorant"
- Client shamelessly flirts with you or your staff
- Patient regularly shares conflict he is having with friends, family, neighbors, colleagues. Often these issues are unrelated to the care issue for which he comes to see you

ANTISOCIAL PERSONALITY DISORDER

Based on the DSM-5, here are the traits most associated with antisocial personality disorder:

- Criminal behavior/difficulty following "social norms," adhering to financial obligations or laws/rules

- Lying/conning
- Impulsive behavior
- Physical altercations
- Remorselessness
- Lack of empathy or concern for others

A timely pop culture example of someone who appears to meet the criteria for antisocial personality disorder is John Meehan, or "Dirty John." If you haven't heard the story about John Meehan, I highly encourage you to check out this real-life example from one or more of the following sources:

- *Dirty John* podcast hosted by *Los Angeles Times* staff writer Christopher Goddard
- *Dirty John* miniseries (originally aired on Bravo TV) starring Connie Britton, Eric Bana, Jean Smart, and Julia Garner
- *Surviving Dirty John*[6] book by Debra Newell and M. William Phelps

John Meehan built his life around abusing and scamming others. Some of his antisocial behaviors included:

- Bilking older adults out of "deposit" money for yardwork he never completed
- Putting glass in his meal at a restaurant so he could sue the establishment

- Misrepresenting himself to ladies he dated and married so he could gain access to the women's finances
- Diverting drugs while working as a nurse anesthetist to support his drug habit and drug-dealing business
- Threatening and physically assaulting others
- Not paying child support for his children

The following are examples of additional red flags you may encounter that signal possible antisocial personality disorder with your clients or patients:

- You repeatedly catch the patient or client in lies
- Patient physically harms you or your staff (or threatens to do so)
- This patient harmed or killed someone accidently (e.g., car accident) but does not express any concern about the injured party or their family

PARANOID PERSONALITY DISORDER

Based on the DSM-5, here are the traits most associated with paranoid personality disorder:

- Believes, without evidence, that others are out to get them
- Regularly doubts loyalty of others
- Difficulty confiding in others

- Finds threats in neutral comments or behavior
- Holds grudges and lacks ability to forgive
- Regularly suspicious about fidelity of spouses or partners without evidence

Here's a case study of someone with paranoid personality disorder traits.

Cory was a thirty-nine-year-old man who struggled with depression and anxiety as well as paranoid personality disorder. It took me many months to establish a good rapport and to properly assess him. Initially, this was because Cory was concerned that I'd break confidentiality or that there were hidden recording devices in my office. After trust was established, Cory shared deep-seated concerns that included:

- being certain his wife was pregnant with his neighbor's child
- worrying that his sister was trying to poison their mother's mind against him
- assuming that his employees were trying to get him fired

During our sessions, Cory could never provide any rationale for these concerns. Despite the lack of evidence, he was wedded to these ideas. Eventually, after referring Cory to a psychiatrist for a medication consult, he "fired" me. The reason: he believed I told the doctor that he was "crazy" and should be "locked up."

The following are example of red flags you may encounter that signal possible paranoid personality disorder in your practice setting:

- Patient suspects you only want to perform surgery for "the money"
- Patient believes you are trying to poison him because of a suggestion to take a prescription medication
- Patient suspects that if she tells you about her health or mental health problems you will tell others who are "out to get her"

DEPENDENT PERSONALITY DISORDER

Based on the DSM-5, here are the traits most associated with dependent personality disorder:

- Pathological need to cling to others for support
- Difficulty being alone
- Obsesses about being unable to care for self
- Extremely indecisive
- Can't take responsibility for life
- Afraid to disagree with others
- Lack of initiative

Here's a case study of someone I worked with who had dependent personality disorder traits:

Joy is a fifty-year-old woman. She's never lived alone and has never been employed. She married her husband at age twenty-two, moving from her parents' home into the marital residence. Although her husband, Don, did not have controlling tendencies, Joy deferred all decisions to him, both small and large. He decided where they'd honeymoon, when they'd have children, and where they'd live. Don made all their financial decisions as well. When Don went on business trips, Joy would insist that one of their parents come and stay to help them with the kids, even when they were teenagers.

Don has recently initiated marriage counseling because his patience with Joy has been exhausted. Now that their youngest child has left for graduate school, they are official empty nesters. Don has been making excuses for Joy's dependency and lack of decisiveness for almost three decades. Joy does not believe there is a problem but is terrified that Don will leave her alone, unable to care for herself.

The following are examples of red flags you may encounter that signal possible dependent personality disorder:

- Client calls you or your staff frequently for no real reason—it seems like this individual just wants to chat

- You discuss treatment options with this patient, and she defers completely to the opinion of her spouse, children, siblings, or friends

- She is not satisfied with your suggestions and recommendations; she insists you tell her what to do

OBSESSIVE COMPULSIVE PERSONALITY DISORDER

Based on the DSM-5, here are the traits most associated with obsessive compulsive disorder:

- Perfectionist tendencies

- Obsessive about rules
- Extreme, inflexible beliefs; black and white thinking
- Hoarding and lack of generosity without good reason
- Difficulty delegating or completing projects

Fifty-year old Jose suffers with obsessive compulsive personality disorder and also has a heart condition.

Although he's extremely bright and ambitious, he has always struggled with completing tasks in a timely fashion at both school and work. Around the office, he's known as the ultimate micromanager. His personality disorder traits were a large contributor to his divorce from his wife. After the divorce, Jose was greatly distressed about the freedom that his ex-wife allowed their teenage kids when they are at her home. Jose does not want his children walking half a mile to school, does not want them spending the night at friends' homes and in general can't tolerate the idea that he doesn't always know what they are doing.

Jose is now a patient awaiting a heart transplant. He has an intricate list of rules about the type of donor he would accept an organ from. He tells his transplant team that he requires that the person be a practicing Roman Catholic, straight, and have a college degree. The transplant team is dumbfounded by this odd behavior and have been trying to convince him that he needs to accept the first match available if he's lucky enough that one comes along.

BACK TO YOU: CLIENTS AND PATIENTS IN YOUR PRACTICE SETTING WHO ARE "ALWAYS DIFFICULT"

After reading the descriptions of these personality disorders, I'm sure you recognize patients and clients (and maybe even some family and friends) who appear to have some of these traits. I imagine they take up an inordinate amount of you and your team's time and energy. Should you diagnose and put a "formal" label in the patient or client's record? That depends on your role and relationship with the individual.

Remember, for many of us—hospital executives, for example—it is not appropriate to formally diagnose what's making this person "difficult." We just want to be aware of those traits.

When we get to Part Three, we are going to cover the strategies you can use to reduce the "hateful" behaviors and increase "grateful" behaviors for clients and patients who exhibit personality disorder traits (as well as those with other mental health conditions). But in the meantime, simply continue to observe your clients and patients. Consider whether you'd put them in the "Usually Reasonable" or "Always Difficult" category.

Clearly there are people who are "Always Difficult" no matter what. But again, that does not mean your Contagious Camaraderie Culture (more on this in chapter 7) can't de-escalate them.

Rick Evans is the senior vice president and chief experience officer for NewYork-Presbyterian Hospital. During our interview for this book, he acknowledged that not every patient will leave theirs or any hospital system *happy*. He has said to his colleagues, "You don't have to make everybody happy, but can we make people feel like, 'I'm in the right place, I'm in good hands?'" Part Three of this book will give you concrete ideas on how to do just that, even for the "Always Difficult."

Learning about personality disorders and some of their identifying traits can help you formulate a strategy to service these particular clients and patients. But before we discuss those strategies, the next chapter will examine the tremendous impact the pandemic and ongoing COVID-19 policies are having on *all* your patients and clients, whether "Usually Reasonable" or "Always Difficult."

CHAPTER 3

How the Pandemic and COVID-19 Policies Have Impacted the Client and Patient Mindset

As a health or mental health professional or leader, you had a front-row seat to the nightmare of the pandemic. While many of you dealt with those who were seriously ill and tragically died, even more of you managed the spinoff effects of seemingly never-ending COVID-19 policies. I'm sure you and your team are still recovering from that traumatic time. You likely experienced some or all of the following:

- Going from "heroes" who received endless pizzas, cookies, and other treats in the early days of the pandemic from patients' family members to being vilified for not doing enough to stop the pandemic

- Constantly changing rules and regulations about adjustments to universal precautions and PPE (personal protective equipment)

- Zoom fatigue from dealing with relentless telehealth appointments because in-person meetings with patients and clients weren't permitted

- Staff walking out or quitting during the early days of the pandemic because of panic

- Major changes to visitor policies

- Worry about your personal health and that of the family you came home to

- Difficulty communicating with colleagues, patients, and clients because of masking policies, particularly with the hearing-impaired, cognitively or mentally challenged individuals, and those who speak a foreign language. (We all got a crash course in how much communication is compromised when facial expressions are hidden and lips can't be read)

- Heated discussions about vaccine mandates

- Being more short-staffed than ever before because of burnout and exhaustion

- Confusion and stress because diverse views about COVID-19 treatment protocols and preventive strategies by seasoned, respected, healthcare professionals were being suppressed. (This censorship was rampant in many healthcare organizations as well as in many media outlets)

- Feeling like you were unable to take time off because your organization was so short-staffed

- The shock and controversy over the criminal conviction of Vanderbilt University Medical Center nurse RaDonda Vaught,[7] who made a medication error in 2017. The court ruling came on the heels of the pandemic when healthcare burnout was rampant and The Great Resignation was well underway

- Trying to pivot from this incredibly difficult last several years under unprecedented and relentless scrutiny

In fact, many of you may still be so busy managing *your* feelings about it that you can overlook that patients (even those not directly impacted by a severe COVID-19 case) have been traumatized as well. In order to transform clients and patients from "hateful" to "grateful," it's imperative to understand the varying perspectives on the pandemic that they have.

COVID-19 and its accompanying policies have had an enormous impact on the way patients, clients, and their families think about healthcare and mental health. For the most part, this tragic time in our history did nothing to further endear patients and clients to the healthcare system. But while most people are even more stressed about engaging with health and mental health providers, this stress has manifested itself differently for everyone.

FEAR

Many people have been immobilized by fear. For some, it was temporary, but for many more, the worry and anxiety has not subsided. Let's briefly review why this happened. Beginning in March 2020, public health messaging emphasized the following:

- COVID-19 can be spread by touching surfaces
- All human beings should stay six feet apart from one another unless they reside in the same household
- People who have no symptoms of COVID-19 are spreading it asymptomatically
- Going out of your home should be minimized as much as possible

Later on, after relentless messaging that wearing a cloth or paper "face covering" or mask was not protective against COVID-19, public health officials changed their tune. Yes, masks should be worn at all times outside the home.

Some of this advice turned out to be not so helpful. Many physicians and healthcare professionals sounded the alarm early on that those most at risk from COVID-19 were the oldest of our population and those with multiple comorbidities. Even the data from the Centers for Disease Control and Prevention (CDC) website confirmed this, but it was rarely discussed by the mainstream media. But even today, there are plenty of people who don't meet these criteria who are still washing their groceries, avoiding friends and family, wearing a mask (even outdoors), and bathing in hand sanitizer. Let's look at an example.

Erin is a healthy twenty-eight-year-old woman. She is absolutely terrified of contracting COVID-19 even though she's been vaccinated. She has no idea that her relative risk for dying or having a poor outcome from this disease is extremely low. She has not had a routine physical examination, dental cleaning, or eye doctor appointment since February 2020. Erin quit her gym membership because she feels being around other sweaty people breathing the same air could prove fatal. Erin does still exercise by walking in her neighborhood, but only at night when she's unlikely to encounter other people. Erin works from home and will only see friends or family members outside with masks on. Erin has received reminder notices from her healthcare providers, encouraging her to make her dentist, eye doctor, and internist appointments, but she is terrified to go into any of their offices.

While the fear of contracting and dying of COVID-19 haunts healthy people like Erin, it can have an even worse impact on those who already struggle with anxiety problems.

Thirty-five-year-old Julie has suffered with obsessive-compulsive disorder and generalized anxiety disorder since her teen years. She has always been disproportionately afraid of germs. Prior to March 2020, Julie's symptoms had been managed well with regular psychotherapy and medication. Unfortunately, the COVID-19 public health messaging has neatly dovetailed with her phobias. Like Erin, Julie is avoiding healthcare offices and social activities. But in addition to washing her groceries, Julie has become compulsive about cleaning her home thoroughly every day. She wears gloves and a mask all day every day, even when tending to her children.

COVID-19 policies have also stoked other fears.

Seventy-seven-year-old Laura was admitted to the hospital during May 2021 for a possible stroke. She arrived via ambulance, and when she got to the emergency department, she had no memory of the ambulance ride. She did not have her cell phone and did not understand why she was at the hospital. After several hours of waiting in the emergency department and not getting answers from staff, Laura was finally admitted to a hospital room. Finally having access to a telephone, she was told by her husband and son what had happened and why she was sent to the hospital. Laura's husband informed her that he attempted to ride in the ambulance with her but was not permitted. He then came to the hospital and was not allowed to enter to wait with Laura in the emergency department. He was also informed that nobody would be allowed to visit her if she was admitted.

Laura spent a nerve-wracking thirty-one hours in the hospital, confused and with no advocate or company. While she reported that the staff were polite and did explain the tests she needed to have, their visits to her room were few and far between. Even just getting access to a glass of water took multiple rings of her call bell. Because of this experience, Laura has become very phobic about the idea of ever returning to a hospital for any reason.

FRUSTRATION

Fifty-one-year-old Karin did everything "perfectly." From March 2020 to March 2022, she only socialized outdoors, worked from home, wore a mask whenever she left the house, got the vaccine, and took all the boosters her doctor suggested. Yet she still tested positive for COVID-19. Twice! She is so frustrated that she did all the "right" things but still got the outcome she so feared. Even though she was only mildly ill the first time she tested positive and asymptomatic the second time, she's exasperated that she couldn't avoid this coronavirus.

ANGER

Others are very angry about the ever-changing messages and sometimes even hypocrisy they've witnessed by public health officials. Many individuals have completely changed their opinions about the safety of hospitals, going to an in-person healthcare provider, assisted living, and utilizing home care services.

Alison's seventy-eight-year-old father died alone in the hospital after a short bout with cancer in May 2020. Nobody in the family was allowed to be with him as he took his last breath. She remembers a nurse calling and putting her father on a speaker phone so she, her sisters, and their children could say goodbye to him. They weren't able to hold his hand or offer him the comfort of their presence. She looks back in contrast to when her mother died in January 2018—the entire family sat vigil in the hospital waiting room round the clock so someone could be with her at all times during the last week of her life. Twelve of them gathered around her to pray as she passed on.

Why, why, why? Alison's bitter anger continues to eat away at her. She remembers pleading with the hospital staff for just one person to be able to visit. She recalls offering for their family members to get tested for COVID-19 and share their results. "Sorry," the hospital said. "That's our policy right now."

Just when Alison thought she couldn't get any angrier, she had a phone call with the funeral home. "Sorry, no funeral. It's against the rules." They suggested she host a memorial on Zoom.

Observing public figures flout the COVID rules during this timeframe only escalated anger among those who experienced a situation like Alison and her family's. There are far too many examples to count of public officials dining out, attending funerals, and enjoying social gatherings. Why was it okay for them to grieve and gather when it wasn't for the rest of us?

Anger has manifested in other ways as well. Sixty-year-old Matthew has an autoimmune disease. He got vaccinated as soon as he was eligible and has received boosters as well. Matthew is furious with his adult son because he and his family did not get vaccinated. In fact, Matthew has taken to social media to express his fury because he feels that irresponsible people like his son are putting him at unnecessary risk. Matthew has gotten into countless virtual battles with Facebook "friends" over this issue.

HOPELESSNESS

John is a single, forty-four-year-old man who lives alone. He moved to a new city right before the pandemic began. He worked in his new office for only three days before it was shut down. His company keeps sending out emails with projections for when they might open the office back up, but there is still no firm date. Because his city has shut down so many times and he doesn't go into an office, John has had a tough time making new friends. He has lost hope that life will ever return to normal.

SADNESS

Seventy-three-year-old Sandy, an assisted living resident, has always been an optimistic person, but she has become quite melancholy since the pandemic hit. She has been glued to the television, watching the death toll. It makes her so sad to know that she's not been able to live fully now that she's finally retired. Visits with family have been less frequent because of COVID waves and their fear that they will infect her. Most other residents in her assisted living community still keep their distance and wear a mask. She misses friendly touches like handshakes and finds it miserable that you can't see anyone's smile.

GRIEF

Eighty-year-old Sharon lost her sister, her husband, and a close friend during the pandemic. Her sister died of COVID-19, but her friend and husband passed away from other causes. She had an in-person funeral for her husband, but very few people attended. There were Zoom memorial services for her friend and sister. While losing three important people in such a short time is always painful, Sharon believes her extended grief is deeper because she was robbed of the usual grief rituals.

LONELINESS

Mike is sixty-five years old. While vaccinated and boosted, he still doesn't feel comfortable socializing much unless it's outdoors. Since he lives in an area with lots of inclement weather, those opportunities are pretty limited. He sees friends on Zoom happy hours, and he plays online chess, but not seeing people "in real life" (IRL, as the kids say) is getting to him.

Thirty-nine-year-old Vince is experiencing loneliness in a different way. He got the first dose of the vaccine and went deaf the day after the shot. Fortunately, his hearing has come back, but he opted not to receive the second dose. He has shared this story with several lifelong friends and family members who have stopped talking to him because they feel he has become an "anti-vaxxer." Vince has been shaken by the mean-spirited things that have been said to him and can't believe that no one showed any empathy about how scary losing his hearing was. Getting cut out of their lives was a complete and total shock. Vince feels completely abandoned by those he loved and trusted the most. He isn't sure whom he can trust with his real thoughts and feelings anymore.

Eighty-year-old Judy doesn't have any kids but has a robust network of friends that she sees at the library, senior center, and for coffee or lunch, often every week. When the pandemic hit, all of her social activities immediately halted. Judy is actually one of the few people in the world who didn't mind her regular doctor's appointments. Although in pretty good health, she had an appointment with at least one of her different providers each month. This too was a big part of her social life. She knew all the receptionists at her doctors' offices and always arrived early to chat with them about their kids and hear stories about what was going on in their lives. During the pandemic, Judy was completely cut off from those healthcare providers and their staff because she didn't have a computer or smartphone. Judy had never felt more alone in her entire life. Regularly she pondered, *Is this really how the rest of my years are going to play out? Completely alone and cut off from other people?*

BURNED OUT

Evan and his husband, Jay, had been taking care of Evan's mom, Gloria, at their home. In July 2019, when Gloria's Alzheimer's disease made it impossible for her to be home alone while they were at work, they enrolled her in full-time adult day care. While the adjustment initially took time, Gloria ultimately flourished at the center. She made friends, participated in music and exercise classes, and was well taken care of by the staff. At the end of every day, Gloria came home tired and slept much better at night than she had in years. The middle-of-the-night wandering that had always woken up the couple and their two elementary school-aged children almost completely ceased.

Fast-forward to March 2020. Evan and Jay are now working from home. Their kids are participating in online "home school." Gloria's adult day care has temporarily closed. Some of the challenges that occurred during this time include:

- Gloria resumed her nighttime wandering, waking up the already stressed household.
- Gloria thought she had to make dinner at 9:45 in the morning when everyone was on their computers. She put a frozen package of ground beef in the oven at 350 degrees. This led to a small fire which could have been deadly if Gloria had been home alone.
- Gloria entered the kids' room while they were at virtual "school," asking them when their deceased grandfather was coming to pick her up. This really upset the children, and they are now afraid there are ghosts in the house.

In my first book, *Cruising Through Caregiving: Reducing the Stress of Caring for Your Loved One*,[8] I encourage adult child family caregivers to emulate the example set by Jay and Evan. While they were committed to keeping Gloria at home, they realized that leaving her alone while they were at work was no longer a safe option. Choosing adult day care can be a powerful decision that provides the older adult suffering with dementia a better quality of life while reducing worry and stress for the rest of the family.

The temporary closing of the adult day care center triggered enormous stress for this family, resulting in burnout for Jay and Evan. Trying to balance jobs, helping their kids with online school, and attempting to manage Gloria's unpredictable behavior proved untenable. Within a month, the couple were at their wits' end. They began snapping at each other and their kids and fighting about how to deal with Gloria. Jay said maybe it was time for assisted living. Evan resisted, saying that it would cost far more than the adult day care did. Also, they had friends who had been denied access to their parents who resided in senior living because of pandemic rules. Evan also worried that Gloria would be more likely to contract COVID-19 if she left home. The news was filled with stories about how older people were sent home from the hospital, infecting others in nursing homes. (While this is true, an assisted living setting is quite different from a nursing home; many laypeople do not recognize the difference.)

They decided to wait it out until the adult day care reopened. After all, the "two weeks to flatten the curve" couldn't last forever, could it? Jay and Evan did the best they could to take breaks from their Zoom calls so they could take walks with Gloria, put on music that she liked, or play a quick game of cards with her. After school, the kids did the same. Everyone powered through, but they were all experiencing burnout. Jay's migraines resurfaced; Evan started developing symptoms of depression. They felt guilty about it, but they all resented Gloria and how hard it was to keep her occupied and "out of trouble." Finally, after all that waiting, in September 2020, the adult day care announced that they were never going to reopen. Evan burst into tears when he heard the news, unsure how they could possibly continue.

SKEPTICISM, DISTRUST, AND CONFUSION

"Two weeks to flatten the curve."

"Actually, we're going to need to lock down longer."

"Wait, this is periodically going to be a regular strategy when 'numbers go up.'"

"Masks don't work. Wait...yes, they do!"

"Vaccines will prevent you from getting COVID-19." "No, actually, they don't! But they will prevent you from getting really sick." "Hold on—well, for some people...others will become hospitalized despite vaccinations."

"One booster is all you need." "Well...actually, you might need two!" "Or maybe even several each year, indefinitely."

And don't even think about asking questions or wanting to see data from the vaccine trials. Doctors, ancillary healthcare professionals, and even laypeople have had their social media accounts suspended or eliminated for asking even basic questions about safety, efficacy, or discussing side effects of the vaccines.

We talked earlier about how many public officials were found to be ignoring the rules during the pandemic. And the messages from trusted organizations like the CDC and local health departments have relentlessly ricocheted all over the place. In fact, 2021's "The Public's Perspective on the United States Public Health System" report,[9] funded by Harvard and the Robert Wood Johnson Foundation, found that only about half of Americans have high confidence in the CDC. Only about one-third report high trust in the NIH (National Institutes of Health) and FDA (Food and Drug Administration). Less than half of Americans have a high degree of trust in their local or state health department. On a positive note, however, this report indicated that about 70 percent of those polled still place high trust in nurses and doctors as well as other healthcare professionals with whom they have a personal relationship. Still, it shouldn't be a surprise that many of your patients and clients will struggle with trusting certain healthcare recommendations since health guidelines and drug approvals come from federal agencies like the CDC and FDA.

There's no question that healthcare and mental health professionals and leaders have been through hell these past several years. But remember that your patients, clients, and their families have experienced their own unique struggles during the pandemic. These experiences are likely to make even those who are "Usually Reasonable" (as discussed in chapter 2) even more difficult to please. But for those who fall into the "Always Difficult" category, be aware that they might be even tougher than ever before.

PART TWO

Why You Should Care About the Mindset of Your Clients, Patients, and Their Families

Part Two will be short and sweet. We discussed at length the mindset of your customers. But now it's time to examine a little more closely why you should care. If you already "get it," you may be tempted to skip this chapter, but please don't—especially if there are those on your team you need to convince that creating a less "hateful" and more "grateful" environment is a win-win for everyone. Let's jump into a brief discussion about what's in it for your patients, clients, and their family caregivers, and what's in it for you and your organization.

CHAPTER 4
What's in It for Them

This chapter will explore the benefits patients, clients, and families enjoy when healthcare leaders and clinicians understand their mindset and strive to transform them from "hateful" to "grateful."

We know that nobody looks forward to any of our services. Nobody wakes up in the morning and says, "Yay! My back hurts—I have to get in with my chiropractor." And of course, as we discussed in chapter 3, the pandemic and COVID-19 policies have exacerbated the stress levels of everyone, including our patients and clients.

So what exactly is in it for them when we understand their mindset and commit to transforming them from "hateful" to "grateful"?

THEY ARE MORE SATISFIED WITH THEIR EXPERIENCE

When you take the time to be nice and understand where your healthcare customer is coming from, they are simply happier with your organization. The 2019 study "Patient-centered communication: dissecting provider communication"[10] was published by Platonova et al. in the *International Journal of Health Care Quality Assurance*. It found that when patients indicated "communication and courteousness ratings were consistent, trust and satisfaction ratings were aligned with these domains."

THEY ARE MORE LIKELY TO SEEK PREVENTIVE CARE

Ideally, healthcare customers will seek our services before there is an emergency. Their problems are easier and cheaper to solve. When they come earlier, there is usually less stress for your clients, patients, and family caregivers.

THEY FEEL EMPOWERED

When you care about the mindset of your patients, clients, and their family caregivers, they feel empowered. In chapter 7, we will hear from Terri Cunliffe of Covenant Living, about their very impressive employee recognition program. Covenant Living provides hospice, in-home care, assisted living, skilled nursing, and rehabilitation services in California, Colorado, Connecticut, Florida, Illinois, Michigan, Minnesota, New Hampshire, Oklahoma, and Washington. A unique aspect of this program is that patients and families are welcome to join in on recognizing exceptional employee service. When employees are recognized, they are eligible for rewards (more on that later). What a sense of power families, patients, and residents must have when they realize that their comments and feedback about how well staff are understanding and treating them can actually lead to tangible rewards for employees!

CHAPTER 5
What's in It for You

It should be pretty obvious that when you transform patients, clients, and family caregivers from "hateful" to "grateful," they will be easier to work with and care for. But let's dig a little further into what we gain and what we avoid. Both are important.

Let's start by talking about what we avoid so we can get that out of the way and end this chapter on a high note!

WE AVOID COMPLAINTS

Look, it's common sense. If we understand the mindset of our customers better and tailor our communication more effectively to them, they will complain less. But let's look at the literature too.

In "Analysis of complaints lodged by patients attending Victorian hospitals, 1997–2001"[11] by David McD. Taylor et al., thirteen million patient complaints were examined over the course of fourteen years. Nearly 30 percent of them were "complaints relating to communication, poor attention, discourtesy, and rudeness." Imagine if you were able to eliminate 30 percent of your complaints! While this study was conducted a while ago, it's a pretty significant one. More recent literature[12] also found that poor customer service is associated with patient, client, and family caregiver complaints.[13]

WE AVOID MALPRACTICE CLAIMS AND LAWSUITS

There is much evidence in the literature that shows the better we are at communicating and providing good service, the less likely we are to face malpractice claims.[14] "Patients who believe that their psychiatrists truly care about their well-being are less likely to sue, even if something goes wrong," says Dr. Paul S. Appelbaum in his article "Malpractice claims in psychiatry: approaches to reducing risk."[15] In the fabulous book *An Epidemic of Empathy*,[16] Dr. Thomas Lee explains that malpractice claims are filed because patients and their families are upset. Lawsuits are correlated with low patient satisfaction.

WE AVOID BAD REVIEWS

In 2019, Dr. Cynthia Liu et al. published "'But his Yelp reviews are awful!': Analysis of general surgeons' Yelp reviews"[17] in the *Journal of Medical Internet Research*. This article examined online Yelp reviews of surgeons in Los Angeles. Did the negative reviews posted focus primarily on clinical outcomes? Nope. The study reports, "As the most common category of complaints was about physician demeanor, surgeons may optimize their Web-based reputation by improving their bedside manner."

Now let's look at what we gain.

YOUR ORGANIZATION GETS TO STAY OPEN

Well, for one, when your culture transforms clients, patients, and family caregivers from "hateful" to "grateful," you get to stay in business. An infamous quote by noted author and speaker Bob Burg sums this concept up beautifully, "All things being equal, people will do business with, and refer business to those people they know, like, and trust." Further, in *An Epidemic of Empathy*, Dr. Thomas Lee says, "Creating an epidemic of empathy is not an act of charity. It is a strategic business imperative." In other words, when we show the patient or client that we genuinely care, our organization flourishes.

YOU'LL GET BETTER REVIEWS

The internet at our house recently went out. And as you know in this day and age, this creates panic for most of us. Never mind that you can't stream television; texting is negatively impacted, and forget about getting any work done on your computer. The cable company that handles our internet sent out a gentleman who spent hours fixing our problem. We kept thanking him, offering him snacks, and telling him how much we appreciated what he was doing. At the end of the visit, he actually gave us his cell phone number! "Don't call the corporate office if you have any more trouble," he said. "Contact me directly." Wow! Amazing service.

He also did something very smart before he left. He told us that the way he was evaluated was based on a text survey that would come to our phone. He reminded us that we had told him several times about how happy we were with his service and added, "Since you feel that way, can you please rate me at the highest score?" And of course, we did. Win-win!

Would we have done that if he'd been indifferent, rude, complained about how stressful his day was, and said that our problem wouldn't be fixed for weeks? No. But he did transform us from "hateful" to "grateful," so he knew we were primed to provide a great review.

You are likely to get a good review when your client, patient, or family caregiver has had a fabulous customer service experience. But you still need to recognize when they are "primed" and make the ask.

"We do make the ask for them to do an online review if they're comfortable in doing so," says Terri Cunliffe, the president and CEO of Covenant Living. I'm guessing that their success in getting online reviews is related to the fact that their patients, residents, and families are actually integral in recognizing good service of staff (which we discussed in chapter 4). They have buy-in!

Leslie Ray, regional director of operations for LCB Senior Living, the second largest provider of senior living in New England, concurs. "You need to ask for online reviews," she says. Ray reports that if you've made the resident or family member's experience a good one, they are likely to honor that review request.

COMPETITIVE ADVANTAGE IN THE MARKETPLACE

There's a reason people flock to institutions like the Mayo Clinic and Cleveland Clinic. They have worked hard to make patient engagement a priority, and they enjoy a competitive advantage in the marketplace. That can be you!

MORE ENGAGED WORKPLACE

Patients, clients, and family caregivers are generally not too happy receiving health, mental health, or senior living services from unhappy staff (more on this in chapter 7). There is an interdependent relationship between the way staff are treated and the way their customers are treated. Organizations that prioritize customer service and patient engagement enjoy a more engaged workplace. Just ask Starbucks, Nordstrom, and the Ritz-Carlton.

PART THREE

Transforming Their Mindset and Experience

The theme of this final—and perhaps most important—section can be summed up by the title of a popular 1993 Toby Keith song: "A Little Less Talk and a Lot More Action." While that tune was about something else entirely, the title describes this last section perfectly. In order to be successful in transforming clients, patients, and their families from "hateful" to "grateful," you need less talk and more action. Show, don't just tell. Having a written mission statement is great. Talking about your fabulous corporate culture is wonderful. Discussing the priority of customer service is fine. But what are you doing to walk the walk rather than simply talk the talk?

CHAPTER 6
Be Who You Say You Are

Let's step out of healthcare for a bit and talk about restaurants. Let's say you are on a business trip and your spouse or partner tagged along to enjoy the resort while you work at a conference. On your last night after you have finished your business, you decide to make a reservation for an upscale date night. You choose a particular steak house because their website and social media pages promise an intimate atmosphere with first-class service, outstanding food, a fantastic wine list, and live romantic music. The prices accompanying their online menu give the impression that this will be a high-end experience. Your choice to dine there is finalized when the concierge at the resort also recommends this steak house based on their reputation and feedback from other guests.

As you wrap up your final long day of work, you are excited about having a relaxing and romantic evening before you head back home on an early flight the next morning. You arrive at the steak house a little early, and your table is not quite ready, so you belly up to the elegant bar. Although the bar is not too busy, the bartender does not acknowledge you immediately. After a few minutes of waiting, you say, "Excuse me, sir," and the bartender whips his head around and says, "What's up?"

"What's up?" might be okay for a sports bar, but you are slightly taken aback. The prices for cocktails, wine, and beer are about three times what they would be in a sports bar. The bartender's remark simply does not match the "promise" of their website, social media presence, or your resort concierge's recommendations. You wonder if you made a mistake by coming to this steak house for your one date night while in this city.

You decide to stick it out, especially since you are observing servers walk by, and the food looks delicious. The host finds you at the bar as you are both finishing a drink and informs you that your table is ready. As you approach your table, you hear the screams of an infant, and several small children are playing on devices with the volume turned up very high. On the other side of your table, a large group of drunk and loud conference-goers is singing along to the live musician playing a Sade song. You ask for a different table but are told there are no other options. Once you are seated, your server comes to the table, and you ask again about another table. He reiterates that there are no other tables but assures you that the table with children should be getting their check soon. The server also assures you that the conference-goers will probably lose steam soon since they've already been at the restaurant for several hours.

Figuring it's way too late in the evening to find another restaurant, and hoping that the experience still might turn around, you decide to go ahead and order. Ten minutes later, the server returns with bread but informs you that your appetizers will take at least an hour because the kitchen is "backed up."

The steak house at this point is just asking to be poorly reviewed on social media because they *told* but did not *show*. Their management should not be surprised that you are going to tell the concierge at your hotel about your disappointing experience. They should expect that your review on social media will not be positive—even if the food is delicious. Much about the actual experience did not align with what you were promised. The bartender's remark, the loud, rowdy atmosphere, and the long wait for food don't match the expectations anyone has when they go to an upscale restaurant.

This does not necessarily mean that there aren't some bar environments where a casual greeting from a bartender would be welcome. It also doesn't mean that kids and loud groups should never be welcome at restaurants. It just means that this restaurant communicates who they are inaccurately, or they are having a very, very off night. If they are truly having an off night, then staffing, codes of conduct for the restaurant, and customer service training need to be revisited. But if this evening's experience is truly their norm, rebranding should be done so diners will have a realistic expectation of the type of experience they will have.

Let's say you do eat at the steak house and the food is incredible. That's not enough because the promised service and ambiance were so lacking. This reminds me of when a clinical outcome is stellar but everyone the patient encountered was rude and unprofessional. The surgery went great, but the bedside manner sucked. The stakes at the steak house (pun intended) are clearly much lower than the stakes at your healthcare organization. But it's the same idea.

Customer experience failures in any industry frequently stem from an organization doing too much *telling* and not nearly enough *showing*. Health, mental health, and senior living fails are no different. When we are clear about what we offer and what a client, patient, or family caregiver can anticipate, expectations are in check. This doesn't mean we won't make mistakes, but it does mean there's a pretty clear line in the sand of what we do and what we don't. It's so important for our customers to know exactly what they can expect from us. And more importantly, it's crucial that we deliver what we say we will. And if we don't, they should have the expectation that service recovery will make them happy again (more on service recovery in chapter 8).

Is your organization really well defined? Does your team genuinely understand who you are and what you offer? Do your clients, patients, and family caregivers know what to expect?

Who are you—really? Is your organization the hospital version of the Ritz-Carlton or a Motel 6? Do residents describe your senior living company as Capital Grille or McDonald's? Is your substance abuse treatment center more comparable to Neiman Marcus or Walmart? Does your physical therapy practice resemble first class or coach? Somewhere in between?

Don't think too hard. What's your gut reaction? Is your organization truly elite, middle of the road, or bare bones? On a scale of zero to ten (zero being bare bones and ten being elite), where would you rate your organization? And what is influencing how you answer this question? It's okay if your organization is middle of the road or bare bones. It doesn't mean that you don't provide a good experience. But if you say you provide an elite experience when it's really bare bones, you will be in for significantly more complaints and dissatisfaction.

That said, an elite hospital is never going to be a Four Seasons hotel. And that's okay. But if you are telling the patients that they will be getting an exclusive experience at your hospital, you need to deliver the Four Seasons version of hospital care. That includes the way staff interact with and speak to the patients, outstanding clinical care, aesthetics, and food.

So how do you do this? You guessed it: You have to *show*, not just *tell!*

When an organization has clarity about what they offer, everything about the organization reflects this: physical space, website, staffing, attire, rates, mission statement, and values.

While it's so important to be who you say you are, it's also important to say how you are different, and to make sure your organization and employees are living that commitment. Here are a couple great examples from my interviewees:

Silverado is a senior living and hospice company specializing in memory care assisted living. They boast only a 3 percent national transfer rate to emergency room, says Jeff Frum, their senior vice president of sales and marketing. If you've ever worked with someone who has dementia, you know how traumatic a visit to the hospital can be. This is such a differentiator, because the national average for transferring assisted living residents to the hospital is approximately 25 percent.

James Lee is the co-founder and CEO of Bella Groves, a San Antonio, Texas, residential and community-based support community for persons living with dementia and their family caregivers. Lee feels that trust and transparency with their clientele is crucial. The Bella Groves website (www.bellagroves.com) *tells* visitors about this value, stating "first and foremost our people build and keep TRUST with one another." Lee shared that one of the ways they *show* that they practice the value of trust is by being completely transparent about their rates by publishing them on the website. Being upfront about fees also distinguishes them from other private-pay organizations offering similar services who don't publish their rates. Lee feels that many organizations choose not to publish rates for a variety of reasons. He believes that ultimately, "Families want transparency; they don't want the explanation for not giving the transparency."

You've got to be consistent and be who you say you are unless there's a really good reason. For example, during the pandemic, many restaurants in countless states were only allowed to provide takeout. Holding an organization to a be-who-you-say-you-are standard during that time would have been very unfair. I know, I know, there are some readers who are thinking, *Maybe restaurants should never have been shut down in the first place*. But regardless of how you feel about pandemic policies and mandates, operations during that time were not always under an individual restaurant's control. It would have been unreasonable for customers to call up in the spring of 2020 and complain that they were unable to get a reservation.

On the other hand, when you change who you say you are with no good reason and without notice, your customers have every right to be upset. And this will contribute tremendously to reduced satisfaction, complaints, and sometimes even to lawsuits.

At the time of this writing, for example, one area where many health, mental health, and senior living organizations are still not back to normal is visitation. Frankly, I hope to God this is all resolved by the time you are reading this book and no patient or client is denied a visitor ever again. Countless family caregivers and their loved ones have dealt with barbaric visitation policies during the pandemic that made no sense. It's perfectly reasonable to not want COVID-19 to spread in your hospital, psychiatric facility, doctor's office, surgical center, nursing home, or hospice facility through visitors. But can't you just ask them to take a rapid test before they see their loved ones? This may not be consistent with the building's longstanding open-door visitor policy, but that would be a sensible workaround to deal with an isolating pandemic mandate.

Let's say you are an upscale drug and alcohol rehabilitation center that touts on its website how important family collaboration is to the healing process. But despite this, you are not permitting family counseling or visits on-site. If you indefinitely continue the no-visitor policy, you are *telling* but not *showing*. Sure, there's Zoom. But life is not meant to be lived indefinitely on Zoom. We all know there is no replacement for hugs, hand holding, and sharing the same physical space as those you love while you are feeling at your most vulnerable. What plans could you implement to restore on-site meetings?

Let's step out of healthcare again. My husband and I lived in a very nice townhome community for many years. One of the benefits of living there was that regular landscaping services were part of our monthly homeowner's fees. Planting, mulching, mowing, weeding, pruning, and other lawncare duties were provided as part of one fixed monthly cost. The landscapers did a beautiful job, and we loved that we didn't have to think about how to make the shrubbery and gardens look beautiful, especially since we both traveled often and neither of us has much of a green thumb. Then, one day out of nowhere, we opened our mail to find a letter citing us for not maintaining our garden and shrubs. *Huh?*

We contacted the property management group; they said that a new policy was in place: homeowners must weed their own gardens and shrubbery. If we didn't clean up the shrubs and flower beds around our home, we would have to pay a fine. We explained that we were never notified of such a policy change.

Ultimately, we found out that association's board of directors never voted on an action to charge a landscaping fee or to fine those who weren't properly weeding their gardens. This new decision was based on the concept that the bylaws of the homeowners' association had been misinterpreted for decades: homeowners should have been weeding their own garden areas for years!

My husband, Sean, who is pretty calm under even the most stressful circumstances, was incensed. He demanded to be informed, in writing, of what constituted "our" garden and shrubbery area versus what was considered the community's. The homeowners' association backed down and dropped their reinterpretation of the bylaws. Very soon after, the landscapers were back to doing their usual fantastic job.

Here's the rub: if the homeowners' association wanted to change the services they were providing, that would have been okay. But that was not the way to go about it. The first step would have been to notify the homeowners in writing that the board would review the issue. Then the homeowners needed to be notified about when that meeting to discuss any changes would be held. Lastly, if the gardening rules were changed, best practice would dictate giving everyone plenty of notice to decide how to handle the change. Would they develop a green thumb or budget extra for the fee?

Perhaps just as importantly, the townhome community would need to overhaul all of their marketing materials. They would need to eliminate the "worry-free maintenance" language from their website and marketing collaterals. It would be important that every potential new resident understood the limits of the landscaping and maintenance and not feel taken advantage of by a hidden fee.

The bottom line is health, mental health, and senior living organizations need to be consistent. If you are the Tesla version of a doctor's office, great. But don't suddenly think it's okay to morph into an old Chevy without notice or explanation. It will be noted by your patients, clients, and their family caregivers. And you'll actually be lucky if they complain to you so you have a chance to fix it. If not, they will likely vent on social media or spread their dissatisfaction through word of mouth. Sometimes you won't hear a peep; they will just take their insurance or private-pay dollars elsewhere.

Being who you say you are is a preventive strategy. The Ritz-Carlton and the Motel 6 both provide you a place to stay, but their branding and messaging communicate the ways they are different, and what you can expect when you choose one of their hotels. The more you can provide a consistent experience that your patients, clients, and family caregivers are expecting, the less time you will have to spend dealing with complaints and poor reviews. Those you serve will be happier, and so will your staff.

Speaking of your team, the next chapter will focus on how to create a culture of "Contagious Camaraderie" where employees *want* to provide great service.

CHAPTER 7

Creating a Contagious Camaraderie Culture: Less "Hateful," More "Grateful" Teams

Moods are contagious. Think about the last time you talked to a friend who was in a horrible mood, complaining about everything that's gone wrong in her life. When you got off the phone with that friend, were you drained or revitalized? Many people—especially empaths—are going to say "drained." But what about when you last talked to your cousin who is hilarious? He made funny observations about everything from pop culture to politicians. He had you laughing practically the entire conversation. Most people would say they were energized by that interaction.

When your staff are miserable, it's a certainty that your customers will feel it. It is also quite possible that they will hear about it. It's pretty much impossible to transform clients and patients from "hateful" to "grateful" if your team feels hateful too. While this is all pretty common sense, much literature supports the theory that happier employees are associated with happier customers.[18]

Denise Manifold is the vice president of sales at Brightview Senior Living, a provider of independent, assisted, and memory care living in eight states. She says that Brightview's ongoing philosophy has been that if you take good care of your team, they will take good care of the residents and their family members. During her thirteen-year tenure, Manifold has observed their executive leadership's (Brightview's partners) down-to-earth engagement with the staff. They are genuinely interested in associate feedback on how to improve the organization. Manifold says that they treat all associates as equals, regardless of their job title or "level" at the organization.

Kevin Goedeke, vice president of regional health operations for Erickson Senior Living, a large provider of continuing care retirement communities in twenty-two states, and the founder of NHA Stand-Up, began working as an administrator in healthcare and senior living when he was just twenty-one years old. "I learned very quickly that you have, as administrators, essentially three customers. One is your employees. Number two are your residents, and number three are the families of your residents. They are all equally important," he says. Heather Guerieri, CEO of Compass, a large nonprofit Maryland hospice, goes even further. While she also considers patients to be customers, employees *and* volunteers fall into that customer category as well. As an aside, she also includes donors and community partners as customers as well.

In the last chapter we talked about being who you say you are and *showing*, not just *telling*. But you also need to show you care about your employees before you can begin to get them to buy into any customer service initiative. Chad Brough, MBA, is the vice president of healthcare transformation at Home Instead Senior Care, an international home care company that provides in-home CARE Pros to help sick and older individuals with activities of daily living. Brough warns that it's a critical mistake to get it backwards. It's essential to improve the experience of the team members before trying to enhance customer service. "Employees really resent you not first fixing the systems and processes that they have to use every day in the delivery of care." At a former organization, Brough helped a healthcare organization's employees "regain the belief that things could be improved." They created a program called "mission control"; at the time, the employees were so disillusioned that they mocked it by calling it "mission impossible."

Brough and his team spent time "soliciting feedback about what was broken from an employee perspective." It was a slow, gradual process, but once they began improving conditions for the employees, team members began to trust that if they shared a concern, it would be addressed. "It was then, and only then, that you could begin having them see different possibilities about the patients that they were caring for." Employees must feel valued and have the tools they need to do a good job before they can even begin to focus on customer service. It's like Maslow's hierarchy (remember I'm a former shrink!). Psychologist Abraham Maslow, of course, discussed the concept that people will make sure they have food and shelter before they concern themselves with finding friends or a romantic partner. The same concept applies to Brough's story.

When you do that, you will have a Contagious Camaraderie Culture which will translate into happier patients, clients, and family caregivers. Let's talk about best practices for making that happen!

CULTIVATE TEAM KARMA: TREAT EMPLOYEES WITH BASIC RESPECT, KINDNESS, COMPASSION, AND EMPATHY SO IT COMES BACK TO YOU AND YOUR CLIENTELE

Let's first define the term "karma." According to Merriam-Webster's online dictionary, one definition is "a characteristic emanation, aura, or spirit that infuses or vitalizes someone or something."

Team Karma is the concept that, when we build up a certain amount of goodwill with our employees, they will be more loyal and work harder for the organization and their manager. They will give you the benefit of the doubt when there is a perceived slight, inconvenience, or disappointment in the workplace. When we treat our team members with kindness, compassion, and empathy consistently, we are typically rewarded with the benefits of Team Karma. Kevin Goedeke of Erickson Senior Living and NHA Stand-Up agrees.

Goedeke believes it's critical to have a foundation of goodwill already built with your team ahead of time. That way, when there are moments where coaching or tough conversations need to happen, the employee is more open to constructive feedback. He likes to ask employees early on what makes their day a happy or sad one. For Goedeke, it's as simple as having twenty minutes to himself for a hot cup of coffee every morning; every employee has some version of that. He thinks it is really important to know the idiosyncrasies for your team members. Goedeke encourages the leaders who report to him to learn about their team members as individuals and to find out why they chose to work with their organization.

I once worked for a healthcare company that did not do a great job building Team Karma with me. They constantly talked about how much they cared about their employees' well-being. But when my grandfather died, that was not my experience.

My Pop died after a short illness. I had been using my vacation time at least monthly to serve as one of his secondary caregivers. When he passed away, I was heartbroken. I had been blessed to live to age thirty without having someone I was extremely close to die. In some ways, the grief stung even more because I was shocked by how painful it was. When I let my boss, Ryan (not his real name), know that my grandfather had died, I told him I would need four days off for the funeral, viewing, and to spend some time with my grandmother. Ryan responded that unfortunately he could only permit me two days off. Even though Human Resources had informed me that I qualified for three days of bereavement leave, and I also had plenty of vacation time to cover those days, Ryan insisted that the two days would be the maximum he'd allow. The reason? There was an internal, out-of-town meeting taking place on two of the days I wanted to be off. He felt my presence at that meeting was absolutely necessary. To add insult to injury, Ryan added that the only way someone could be excused from this meeting was if they'd requested the time off well ahead of time. As if I could plan when my grandfather was going to die.

Well, I attended that mandatory meeting and I was a zombie. I cried every night in my hotel room. I finally broke down and told one of my colleagues about my grandfather dying right before the trip, and she was upset on my behalf. She said I should've pushed back and refused to attend. I responded that I was concerned that if I had done that, my boss would have found a way to fire me. I was intimidated by his lack of empathy for my grief. At the time, I didn't financially feel like I could lose my job without having another one lined up.

But after going through the motions at that out-of-town meeting, I made the decision that I was going to find another job. I couldn't work for someone who clearly did not care about me as a person.

Do you think I was offering my best to our healthcare customers between the time I lost my grandfather until I found another job? I would never have intentionally treated any client poorly or unprofessionally, but I know I was coming to work every day feeling dejected. Sure, I was still grieving, and that was part of my less happy mood. But grieving while knowing you've been taken care of by your employer during a tough time is always going to be easier than when you feel they've dismissed your loss. I can't imagine that my performance and customer service during that time didn't falter at least a little bit. In contrast, when my father-in-law passed away, my husband Sean's manager told him to take as much time as he needed. My husband is still at that same company to this day.

What would have happened if I simply had been excused from that meeting? I've thought about it a lot over the years. The Team Karma from that action would've been monumental.

Increased loyalty and appreciation for my boss and employer would have been the most likely outcome. I can't imagine that I'd have been out looking for a new job. Likely, I would've been encouraging others to apply at an organization that treated their team members so well.

I did share my disappointing experience with a couple of trusted colleagues; they could tell I was not quite myself in the weeks that followed this incident. An employee feeling unsupported when a family member dies does not typically go over well with their coworkers when the organization's messaging is all about helping people who are sick, caregiving, and grieving. That's bad enough on its own. But what happens when healthcare employees discuss their lousy workplace culture with patients and clients? All identifying names and details of the following true story have been changed.

I'd been seeing Dr. Bell for over a decade at Desert University Primary Care, a very prestigious medical practice affiliated with an even more impressive teaching hospital. Dr. Bell is the gold standard of physicians. Not only was she educated at the very best schools and a great diagnostician, but she also had a compassionate bedside manner and provided personalized, individual care. Both she and her longtime medical assistant, Joy, also had great personalities. Chatting with both Joy and Dr. Bell during my annual visits made the experience of going into a healthcare appointment very comfortable.

During my final visit to Desert University Primary Care, Joy came into the room to take my vital signs without her usual smile. When I asked what was wrong, she said, "I wanted to be sure you knew that Dr. Bell is leaving the practice." Assuming that Dr. Bell got a great offer from somewhere else, I asked where she was headed. Joy responded that Dr. Bell's husband had become very ill and was now terminal. She had been using Family Medical Leave Act (FMLA) days to take care of him. Because she'd used up all her time, she requested to work part time through the rest of her husband's illness. The practice managers told her that policy stated they could only employ full-time physicians.

Joy went on to say that she could not wrap her head around how short-sighted their bosses were being. Joy listed all of Dr. Bell's incredible qualities and said that she couldn't believe the practice would rather lose a great, longtime doctor than have a part-time one. She also expressed disgust at the fact that this renowned medical practice that was allegedly so "caregiver-friendly" could be so cold to someone who was caregiving in her personal life. Further, Joy shared that she tried to rally other employees in the practice to stand up for Dr. Bell but they wouldn't. She told them, "If this can happen to a longtime, outstanding employee like Dr. Bell, it could happen to any of us."

I felt more and more disappointed as Joy went on. She knew I'd authored a book on caregiving, so I guess she felt she could confide in me. But maybe she was telling this story to all their patients—who knows? While Joy probably shouldn't have aired the "dirty laundry" of this organization, I understand why she did. Not only was she losing a colleague and friend, she was also incensed about the hypocrisy she was witnessing in a workplace she used to respect.

As you can probably guess, I stopped patronizing this practice. I also wrote a review letting them know how disappointed I was with what I'd heard. This one story from a trusted employee about this practice changed my view about them completely. And never mind the fact that it's next to impossible to find doctors who want to practice primary care anymore!

My company, Jenerations Health Education Inc., is far from perfect. But when I began it, I knew that I wanted our Contagious Camaraderie Culture to be one of taking care of each other and showing compassion when someone had a serious personal situation. Allow me to share with you just a few examples of how our former and current team members have stepped up for one another.

When my grandmother died, my team members Stephanie Goldstein and Dr. Ann Morrison filled in at speaking engagements. When our associate speaker Mary Fridley's father-in-law passed away, our team went out of their way to cover her events. A week after Dr. Morrison's mother passed away, she didn't feel up to attending our annual team meeting. We all supported her, trusting that she knew how best to take care of herself during that difficult time. When associate speaker Joanna Frankel got COVID-19, everyone pitched in to make sure her events were covered. When my father dropped dead unexpectedly, associate speaker Cathy Brock actually drove one hundred miles to support me by paying her respects at his memorial service *on her birthday!*

This is not to say that we don't have "non-negotiables" at Jenerations. Whenever someone joins our team, we emphasize our two major "rules":

- Though you can make your own schedule, if you commit to an event as a speaker or moderator, it's yours unless you can find a substitute. Of course, as I just described, if there's a true emergency (death, serious illness, etc.), we will take care of everything for you

- Be nice and professional to each other and our customers

But that's pretty much it. Yes, there's a lot of other stuff that's required for us to do our jobs well, but the two above "non-negotiables" are most important. But as you can see from the examples I shared about how we cover for each other when there's a real emergency or tragedy, organizations can have "rules" and still be caring and compassionate.

Another important example is the way we treat employees who are sick. Before the COVID-19 pandemic entered our lives, it was socially acceptable to go to work ill. It's less so now, but the phone call of a sick employee is still one of the most dreaded. Leslie Ray, regional director of operations for LCB, says the way we treat employees when they call out sick tells the employee a lot. When leaders hear the phrase "I'm sick," they usually stop listening and being present with the employee. Yes, you need to replace that nurse on the shift. But it only takes a moment to say, "I sure hope you feel better. Take good care of yourself."

Cara Silletto, MBA, CSP, is the author of *Staying Power: Why Your Employees Leave and How to Keep Them Longer*[19] and the founder of Magnet Culture, a company that helps organizations reduce employee turnover. Silletto thinks it's really important for us to thank our employees very regularly. Heather Guerieri, CEO of Compass, feels the same. She thanks her employees daily and encourages her leaders to thank their teams every day too.

I am sure there are some leaders reading this who are saying to themselves, "Seriously? Thank them for coming in? They are supposed to come in! This is their job, and we pay them!" But let's consider the example Leslie Ray shared about an employee calling in sick. Aren't we thankful when they *don't* call in sick? Aren't we glad we don't have to find someone to fill in at the last minute? A simple "thank you for coming in," as Silletto suggests, could potentially go a long way to reducing call outs. The bottom line is that nobody ever *has to* come in! Particularly during The Great Resignation, people left health, mental health, and senior living jobs in droves.

TREAT EMPLOYEES LIKE THEY HAVE A LOT OF OTHER JOB OPTIONS...BECAUSE THEY DO

Speaking of The Great Resignation, let's talk about whom to retain before we talk about whom to hire! We all know it's much better and less expensive to keep a good employee rather than hire a new one. Keeping good people in the right positions is crucial to developing a Contagious Camaraderie Culture.

There has been a staffing shortage in health and mental healthcare for a very long time. I personally have been stressed out about it for years, particularly when I think about the explosion of the aging population. For at least a decade, I've wondered, "Who will take care of all of us?" One of the reasons I've been so committed to teaching at Johns Hopkins Certificate on Aging program is because it's an opportunity to mentor students who are interested in transitioning to health or mental health careers in geriatrics or gerontology.

Obviously, the pandemic intensified these staffing shortages. Many health and mental health leaders are working tirelessly to make their workplaces as appealing as possible. But unfortunately, some just don't get it. They still act like their employees are lucky to have a job.

Healthcare, senior living, and mental health organizations are always competing with other healthcare, senior living, and mental health organizations for clinicians, for sure. Doctors, physical therapists, social workers, psychologists, certified therapeutic recreation specialists, music therapists, and nurses will look for other opportunities with your direct competitors. But non-clinicians who are also essential to health, mental health, and senior living businesses have many, many more options.

Your best human resources, maintenance, public relations, housekeeping, fundraising, sales, marketing, IT, accounting, and other staff can get jobs in almost any other industry.

But what about those who are committed to your field but aren't making a lot of money or seeing much opportunity for career growth, like direct care staff. Certified nursing assistants (CNAs), for example, make approximately twenty dollars per hour as of this writing. Yes, healthcare paraprofessionals have received training and are frequently quite committed to their jobs. Ask the best CNAs why they wanted to work in a nursing home or hospital. They will likely cite their compassion for others, a nurturing personality, and experience taking care of loved ones in their families. But their job is one of the toughest ones on the planet. They wipe butts, get spit on, and generally do all the "unskilled" work that a doctor or nurse is too busy to do. When they don't feel appreciated, yes, sometimes, they will go to a competitor. But they also might think about leaving the industry completely. They can make the same amount of money—and maybe even have better benefits and schedules—going to work at a fast-food establishment, a hotel, or a grocery store.

If your pharmacy provides the chance to earn a college scholarship, you are probably going to be in a better position to recruit from local high schools than your competition. But if you don't have the budget for that, it's okay. What else can you do to show high school students that you would value them if they came to work with you? Perhaps you could ensure them during the recruitment process that you will work around sporting events and final exam schedules.

Have you ever considered letting employees bring their kids to work? While this certainly isn't appropriate for every practice setting, it works beautifully for Silverado. Jeff Frum, their vice president of sales and marketing, says letting kids come to work has been win-win-win for their organization. Their cognitively impaired residents enjoy spending time with kids, the kids make lasting memories, and the employee parents don't have to find childcare. Policies like this endear working parents to the organization. Silverado was kind enough to allow me to print their associate children visitation policy here in case you'd like to emulate it.

Silverado's Associate Children Visitation Program

- It is the practice of Silverado to support associate families as much as possible by allowing associates to bring their children to work with them. Bringing a child to work is a privilege and not a right.

- One of our core values is to retain and build family unity with our residents and their loved ones. This also includes Silverado associate families too. Having children visit our residents gives our residents opportunities to nurture others and moments of spontaneity. Over the years we have learned that this practice is a huge benefit to the children too. We have heard from many of our Silverado children that it was because of their experience with the residents that inspired them to become doctors, teachers, nurses, etc., and that they also learned to be helpful, empathetic, and respectful of those who have physical and cognitive challenges.

- Parent associate must be able to supervise their child (children) without the interference of their job responsibilities.

- To support the Parent associate, the Engagement Director will plan activities during the day that will involve interactions of residents with children.

—Reprinted with Permission from Silverado

I once worked for a narcissistic boss who actually told me that she believed it was good for employees to always be afraid they will get fired. Clearly, I disagree with that. There are certainly instances where an employee is no longer a good fit or has done something egregious that requires their employment must be terminated. But employees who are worried that you will fire them on a whim, or who don't believe you recognize their value on the open market, are not doing their best work for your patients and clients.

Cara Silletto, founder of Magnet Culture, says many organizations focus vigilantly on recruitment but pay much less attention to retention. She recommends that organizations divert some funds that would be spent on a recruiter to a "retention specialist." This person works alongside hiring managers and leaders to ensure that new hires feel welcome, are getting properly oriented, and that any early kinks are worked out. Silletto gave me permission to share Magnet Culture's sample retention specialist job description:

RETENTION SPECIALIST

Sample Job Description

Created and Provided by Magnet Culture,
Copyright 2022

The primary roles of the Retention Specialist are to determine why people are leaving the organization and build relationships and initiatives to extend employee tenure.

Job Responsibilities

- gathering qualitative retention data by conducting and analyzing employee surveys and/or stay interviews
- building employee networks/committees
- serving as an employee ambassador for staff to ask questions and provide feedback
- ensuring the onboarding process is welcoming, thorough, and incorporates the company culture

- determining gaps where additional supervisor/ management training is needed
- coordinating (and possibly conducting) supervisor/ management training and development programs
- identifying operational/system changes that help adjust to a shorter-term workforce
- analyzing compensation and scheduling for models that better align with today's workforce's needs
- developing innovative opportunities for advancement and career paths for workers
- implementing recognition and appreciation programs across the organization
- ascertaining ways the organization and managers can be more transparent with employees
- developing effective staff meeting schedules, agendas, and tools for those leading meetings
- crafting organizational messages that instill the company's mission and core values
- revamping the interview process, selection criteria, and applicant communication plan
- creating more realistic job preview opportunities for candidates

- improving the employer brand outside the organization within the community
- working with all leaders to make the organization a better place to work

SAMPLE Requirements

- Must love people
- Must love continuous improvement
- Must have excellent verbal and written communication skills
- Must understand the way business has been done as well as how it is evolving over time
- Must have a diplomatic demeanor to effectively resolve conflict
- Must be able to gather, organize, and analyze data
- Must be able to create plans, processes, and checklists
- Project management experience preferred
- Training and/or leadership coaching skills preferred

SAMPLE Goal

> Success in this role will be determined by the improvement in employee retention across the organization measured against the initial trajectory of company statistics.
>
> *—Reprinted with Permission from Magnet Culture*

HIRE NICE PEOPLE WHO GET ALONG AND "GET IT"

Leslie Ray, regional director of operations for LCB, says she doesn't believe in the adage that we don't have to like the people we work with. She believes work is much more pleasant when we enjoy our colleagues. In fact, when she was interviewing with LCB, she was extremely impressed that they tried really hard to get to know her as a person and not just as a potential candidate. They said to her, "We know you can do the job, based on your credentials, but we want to know you as a human being." She also loves that they call their employees "family" rather than teammates or associates.

I talked a little bit before about my two non-negotiables at Jenerations. And frankly the most important one is that we only bring on nice people who we know will get along with everyone else on our team and with our customers. Look, when we add someone to our speaking roster, we want to be sure that the person meets the educational requirements for teaching certain material. We need to be sure the speakers have an engaging style and are going to be reliable when they accept gigs. When we hire administrative staff, they need to possess certain technical skills. But most importantly, for everyone who works on our team, my expectation is for them to be nice.

Allan Anderson, MD, MBA, is a geriatric psychiatrist, director of Banner Alzheimer's Institute at Banner Health in Tucson, Arizona, and former assistant professor of psychiatry at Johns Hopkins University. Dr. Anderson says that at Banner, they insist on hiring people that have "it." The "it" he's referring to is passion to work in their field.

Daniel Blum is the president and CEO of Sinai Hospital of Baltimore and Grace Medical Center and senior vice president at LifeBridge Health. He says that boards of healthcare organizations need to be clear on what they want in a chief executive. "Do they want somebody who's going to be a ruthless businessperson and produces much margin on an annual basis above everything else? Or do they want somebody who is going to assure the financial success of the organization, but at least in equal measure take into consideration things like culture and other performance metrics?"

INCLUDE BOUNDARIES IN YOUR CULTURE

Professional boundaries are the invisible line between the employee and the patient, client, or family caregiver. Most licensed health and mental health professionals receive at least some education about boundaries in school. That said, some disciplines are stricter about them than others. For example, psychologists, psychiatrists, social workers, and other professional counselors have very firm rules about "dual relationships." Dual relationships occur when the social worker, psychologist, or psychiatrist is not just serving the client as, say, a therapist, but he also has the client over for cookouts since they have become close friends too. This is a big no-no. Professionally serving personal friends and family members is also deeply frowned upon by the psychiatric, psychological, social work, and related communities. Of course, the most egregious dual relationship offense in these professions is either professionally treating someone with whom you are sexually or romantically involved, or beginning a sexual or romantic relationship with a current patient or client. Some of these transgressions can lead to suspension and loss of licenses.

Many other healthcare professionals have guidelines about dual relationships, but they tend to be looser. It is the responsibility of each individual licensed health and mental health professional to follow their own state regulations with the support of their organization. But it's also important for leaders to realize that many people who work in your organization have had absolutely no training about dual relationships and don't hesitate to become friends or romantic partners with your patients and clients. The question is are you okay with that?

Alex works in billing at your hospital. He met Kelly while she was accompanying her father to chemotherapy appointments. They have begun dating and it's gotten serious. Now, Alex is attending family meetings with your hospital staff. It is getting very awkward as your clinical and administrative staff feel Alex is "throwing his weight around" and acting as though he has power over them.

Is this something your organization is comfortable with? Unless you have specific policies about fraternization, it will not occur to many of your employees that they shouldn't become friends with or date your patients, clients, and their families. For many employees, especially those who work in administrative, maintenance, dietary, housekeeping, billing, and other ancillary departments, the idea that fraternization could lead to workplace drama is not on their radar screen. Even if the person is highly seasoned and very skilled!

Joe works as the director of culinary services at an extremely expensive, high-end senior living community. Having been educated at Le Cordon Bleu in Paris, his prior experience includes working at Michelin-star restaurants and as a personal chef. Joe does an amazing job; the residents and families love his food, he takes food safety and kitchen hygiene extremely seriously, and his staff think he's an amazing boss.

You know you have been extremely lucky to have Joe on board for the last three years.

Over the last eight months, Joe has bonded with one of your new independent living residents, Ben. Ben really reminds Joe of his uncle who died recently. Both Joe and Ben are widowed, Italian, enjoy golf, and love the Boston Red Sox. They have even played golf together and gone to a few baseball games.

Some of you might be reading this and applauding Joe. This is a great employee who is going above and beyond—we encourage this sort of engagement! But some of you might believe it can lead to a problem. In this case it did.

The other residents are observing this relationship and becoming a bit jealous. One of them heard that Joe learned how to make *cacio e pepe* using Ben's deceased wife's recipe. One of the members of your resident council is complaining that Ben is getting special treatment and it's not fair.

Some of your staff are irritated too. In a very elite, expensive senior living community where many residents are extremely rich, Ben is widely known to be one of the wealthiest. Rumors are going around that Joe is buddying up to Ben so he will be remembered in his estate.

When you share these concerns with Joe, he is shocked and insulted. He can't believe that anyone would be upset with him befriending an old man with whom he shares a number of common interests. But you feel like Joe needs to have better boundaries for the good of the community, for both the staff and residents.

When Joe expresses how offended he is by the gossip and says that it's ridiculous, would you really be surprised? He can't see that he's done anything wrong. He's never had anything but A+ inspections from health department surveyors. Residents, guests, and staff rave about his meals and snacks. Why are you just bringing up for the first time that there's a limit to how friendly you want staff to become with the residents? Over the course of his career in hospitality, Joe has befriended countless customers, and no organization ever had an issue with it.

So, who is right here? If Joe was never told that he shouldn't socialize outside of work with the residents, it really isn't fair to blame him. His professional ethics don't preclude him from hanging out with Ben. In fact, the United States Personal Chef Association's code of ethics states that chefs will have: "respect for the client's home, property, belongings, and privacy, always acting discreetly and *as a member of his/her family.*" Although Joe is not currently functioning as a traditional personal chef, he is cooking for individuals in their home. He's confused: should he not treat the residents as family? After all, his senior living company is constantly spouting that they are so proud of their "family environment."

Your organization needs to be clear on where the lines are so a Contagious Camaraderie Culture is maintained. This is especially true for those staff who don't have specific boundaries required by their licenses. Having good, reasonable professional boundary standards *specific to your practice setting* is one of the most proactive ways you can prevent problems in your organization. It's up to your leadership (and in some cases, your legal team) to create ones that make sense for your organization. And they must be communicated early and often, in writing and during training classes. You can't rely on all your team members to follow the same boundaries in a multidisciplinary setting unless they are told exactly where the lines are in your organization.

We saw the issue that occurred when Joe wasn't clear on your organization's boundary preferences. What other problems can good boundary practices prevent? Burnout, compassion fatigue, and countertransference. These are some of the top enemies of a Contagious Camaraderie Culture and a more "grateful" patient/client environment.

Burnout, compassion fatigue, and countertransference can occur when a team member doesn't have good boundaries with the client, patient, or family caregiver. But they can also occur when a team member doesn't have good boundaries with their manager, colleagues, and organization.

I can't imagine there's a single reader of this book who is unfamiliar with burnout since the pandemic. But let's define it anyway so we're all on the same page.

According to the World Health Organization (WHO) website, "Burnout is a syndrome conceptualized as resulting from chronic workplace stress that has not been successfully managed. It is characterized by three dimensions:

- feelings of energy depletion or exhaustion
- increased mental distance from one's job, or feelings of negativism or cynicism related to one's job
- reduced professional efficacy"

Further, in 2019, the eleventh revision of the International Classification of Diseases (ICD-11) began listing burnout as an "occupational phenomenon."

Dr. Naim El-Aswad is the chief medical officer at Vital Signs Vital Skills LLC, and the recently launched Warrior Recovery Center based in Texas. He is also the author of *Physician Burnout: An Emotionally Malignant Disease.*[20] To Dr. El-Aswad, the *correlation* between burnout and low patient satisfaction is very clear. He says clinician burnout impacts what the patient both *feels* and *knows*. "The patient needs to feel safe, and the patient needs to be able to trust the person in front of them." He says the patient also needs to "know that you are competent; they have to know that you care."

Dr. Arif Kamal, the chief patient officer for the American Cancer Society and associate professor of medicine and population health at the Duke University School of Medicine, concurs. Dr. Kamal shared that when he mentors physicians about how important it is that they express that they care about their patients, some providers are taken aback. They respond with, "Of course I care about them; I'm their oncologist." But particularly when a provider is burned out, the fact that they care may not be obvious to the patient.

When people interact with one another, "they interact on three axes: cognitive, behavioral, and emotional," Dr. El-Aswad says, and burnout impacts all of these. Advanced brain imaging technology (SPECT) demonstrates that when a person is experiencing burnout, there are "functional holes" in the prefrontal cortex of the brain. How is this relevant to clinical practice? Dr. El-Aswad explains that prefrontal cortex dysfunction can include challenges with concentration, decision-making, and judgment. Since the prefrontal cortex is also responsible for our ability to control impulses, feel empathy, optimism, and insight, the problems that impact the patient are countless. Errors, behaving unprofessionally and unethically, as well as poor communication are likely to occur. And of course, not only does this impact clinical outcomes, it also obliterates bedside manner and patient engagement. "In order to be ethical, you have to have the ability to understand the difference between right and wrong." Sadly, the phenomenon of burnout interferes with this.

Let's talk about all those staff who worked countless days in a row during the pandemic. Maybe they were told that they couldn't take off; maybe they perceived that they couldn't take off. "Burnout is twelve stages, and we oscillate between those twelve stages. We can have days when we are burned out but are under control...we have days when we are not in control and the burnout is manifesting itself rampantly," says Dr. El-Aswad. Maybe an employee worked seventy-five days in a row and is burned out. It may be obvious on some days but less so on others.

Dr. El-Aswad says it's courageous to acknowledge and understand burnout. Dr. El-Aswad shared that he once worked with a C-suite healthcare leader who said, "I can't afford to know who's burned out," because this executive didn't want to be judged if people knew he was allowing burned-out clinicians to work! Would you want to receive your care at this institution?

Dr. El-Aswad says that an organization doing a good job with preventing and managing burnout is acknowledging that it exists and that it is "on their list of priorities." In fact, some organizations are beginning to create chief wellness officer (CWO) positions, he says. When that person is competent, the organization has a real chance at conquering burnout and the impact it has on staff, clinical outcomes, and ultimately customer service. Of course, many smaller organizations can't necessarily afford a chief wellness officer. But in lieu of that, simply communicating to team members that they need to let you know where their line is and that it will be respected is quite impactful in many practice settings. Dr. Kamal of the American Cancer Society recommends that healthcare leaders meet with their teams to discuss the emotional challenges of the work. Dr. Kamal suggests this conversation starter: "This work is hard. This is what makes it hard for me..." Then team members can feel comfortable being vulnerable with their struggles.

When I asked Dr. El-Aswad what a brand-new organization starting from scratch could do to prevent, minimize, and manage burnout, he informed me that he was about to open a new facility where he will be able to do just that! At the time of this writing, he and his team just launched a PTSD (post-traumatic stress disorder) and substance use disorder treatment center for veterans. The Warrior Recovery Center in Houston provides a residential and partial hospitalization program and intensive outpatient services to veterans. Eventually there will be a sober living component as well.

Here's his strategy for preventing burnout in his new venture:

- Make sure all employees know about and understand burnout
- Create a safe environment where burnout can be discussed

- Identify resources to help employees if they feel burned out
- Keep evaluating if people are burned out
- Provide interventions at the organization if burnout does occur
- Provide continuous support

Less frequently acknowledged by healthcare leaders are what I call burnout's ugly cousins: compassion fatigue and countertransference.

Merriam-Webster's online dictionary defines compassion fatigue as: "...the physical and mental exhaustion and emotional withdrawal experienced by those who care for sick or traumatized people over an extended period of time. / Unlike burnout, which is caused by everyday work stresses (dealing with insurance companies, making treatment choices), *compassion fatigue* results from taking on the emotional burden of a patient's agony—Tim Jarvis."

Let's talk a little bit about compassion fatigue. According to the American Institute of Stress website, it is defined as "the emotional residue or strain of exposure to working with those suffering from the consequences of traumatic events." A second definition, from Merriam-Webster's online dictionary, says that it's "apathy or indifference toward the suffering of others as the result of overexposure to tragic news stories and images and the subsequent appeals for assistance."

Lindsay, a hospice nurse, began to experience signs of compassion fatigue and burnout during November 2020. Lindsay was pretty stressed out during the beginning of the pandemic as her employer did not have sufficient PPE (personal protective equipment). After visiting dying patients and their panicked family members in their homes every day, she'd come home, take a shower, put her clothes right in the washer, and sleep in her daughters' room without seeing the rest of the family. Lindsay's wife, Pam, and their daughters would sleep together in the couple's room to prevent anyone from getting sick if Lindsay were to bring COVID-19 home.

Over the next several months, many other stressors built up as well. Several of Lindsay's team members quit, so she did not feel like she could take her days off, her daughters were doing home school, and Pam got laid off from her job as a hotel manager. Lindsay felt like she was holding it together pretty well until one of her favorite cancer patients, Jessie, a thirty-year-old mother of a toddler, died. While driving home from the patient's home after pronouncing her dead, Lindsay realized that she felt numb. She always felt *something* when she lost a patient, especially a young one that she really liked. She had just seen too much death and trauma in the last seven months—some of it from COVID-19, but most of it from other terminal illnesses.

It was a perfect storm. Personal stressors. Only having taken off three days in the last seven months. Those factors, combined with the relentless death and grief she faced at work, combined with the continuous loop of deaths and cases scrolling across her television set every night, rendered Lindsay indifferent. When Lindsay began to see me for private coaching, she told me that she found herself just not caring about her patients anymore. She knew something was wrong with her, but she didn't even feel bad about not caring.

Prior to this experience, Lindsay's boss, colleagues, and Lindsay herself would have described her as an incredibly empathic and caring nurse. So what could have protected Lindsay from compassion fatigue and burnout? Clearly, the pandemic happened to everyone, including every healthcare professional. The home school stressors happened to a lot of parents. Many partners and spouses of healthcare workers lost jobs before Paycheck Protection Program money was available. That was out of her control. But what could Lindsay control? What would have been protective against compassion fatigue? Boundaries.

I'm sure there are some of you reading this thinking that the compassion fatigue and burnout she experienced was inevitable. And maybe it was. For some people it would be. But if Lindsay put an invisible line up between herself and her patients by saying to her manager, "I must take more time off for my physical and mental health," she likely would have suffered less. Or, she could have said, "I need to refer out some of my most distressing cases because I can't handle the vicarious trauma."

I speak and write about boundaries a lot because I firmly believe that good boundaries prevent a lot of problems. Sometimes it makes people mad because they'll say that somebody like Lindsay had no choice. But we always have a choice.

I bet Lindsay's manager, Donna, was initially thrilled that she didn't push for more time off or for a less traumatizing, less stressful caseload. They needed her to work because they were short-staffed and they had a lot of very needy patients and families that required care. It was one less thing her manager had to worry about during a very stressful time as a healthcare leader.

But Donna was no longer thrilled when a Google review was brought to her attention by a corporate executive. Although the review was anonymous, it was clearly from Jessie's husband, and without naming the hospice employee, it was obviously about Lindsay. He described how devastating it was to deal with his young wife's short illness and how he felt she got shortchanged because of the pandemic. He went on to say that the nurse who came to the house on the day Jessie died barely offered her condolences.

Donna was startled by this. Lindsay was one of her best. Yes, the pandemic had taken its toll on everyone, but she just couldn't believe Lindsay would have been so cold to a patient's family. Donna could only imagine that the husband had misunderstood; it had to have been because of the personal protective equipment. During the pandemic, many hospice nurses were going into patient's homes looking like they were from outer space because of all the PPE they were required to wear. Not only is this type of attire extremely physically uncomfortable, but it also creates an obvious communication barrier. Even if Lindsay had been at her most centered on the day she pronounced Jessie deceased, some of the human connection would have been lost. But Donna is taken aback when she shares the feedback with Lindsay. Lindsay says she no longer thinks she is cut out for hospice work and is going to give her two weeks' notice.

When employees allow management and leadership to push through their wellness boundaries, nothing good comes of it. I'm not saying it's Donna's responsibility to know exactly what her employee's frame of mind is at every minute of the day. But when an employee has only taken three days off in more than half a year, it's bound to take a toll. In the short term, having workhorse employees seems like a gift from heaven. But ultimately the organization, the employee, the patients, and their families pay the price. In this circumstance, it was a case of compassion fatigue and burnout.

Should Lindsay have been more proactive? Of course. She should have insisted that she needed a break. Working in hospice is exhausting and daunting under normal circumstances, but during the pandemic it was downright grueling. I would guess that Lindsay—like many others during the pandemic—got into a bit of martyr complex. She may have believed that if she took days off, everything would fall apart for her patients. This is a very dangerous mindset because no employee should ever feel like they are "the only one" who...(fill in the blank). But when management normalizes extreme hours and high-intensity caseloads and working conditions, that's exactly what they are encouraging. And compassion fatigue and burnout are common outcomes.

Countertransference may be even less well understood than compassion fatigue. Generally, only psychotherapists are familiar with the term. But I swear, everyone in every industry goes through some version of this at work—especially healthcare professionals and leaders.

What exactly is countertransference? According to the American Psychological Association Dictionary of Psychology, countertransference is "...the therapist's unconscious (and often conscious) reactions to the patient and to the patient's transference. These thoughts and feelings are based on the therapist's own psychological needs and conflicts and may be unexpressed or revealed through conscious responses to patient behavior."

Countertransference happens to everyone. Nobody is immune. Again, I want to emphasize that while countertransference is not a term that is frequently used outside of a shrink's office, it should be. When someone has a strong emotional reaction to the client, patient, or family caregiver, countertransference is probably happening. Maybe working with the client is making you feel angry, scared, exasperated, stupid, lonely, incompetent, foolish, you name it. But it doesn't necessarily have to be a negative emotional reaction. It can be a pleasant one. Maybe you really like a client or patient. Maybe you feel overly protective about the patient—much more so than you do with other patients.

Some counselors and psychotherapists tend to think of countertransference in simple terms. This client looks just like my abusive ex-husband, so I need to be extra careful that I don't treat him differently. The therapist's natural reaction around this client is to cower and avoid eye contact, for example. She talks it through with her supervisor, and they work on strategies so she can remain objective and confident with the client. Or in some cases, they might together decide that this client would be better served by another therapist. This is overt countertransference. What's harder to recognize is covert, less obvious countertransference.

Let me give you an example. When I was a psychotherapist, I worked with a retired older adult man named Thomas, who was paying his fifty-year-old son's rent and other bills. The son was able-bodied and could work but chose not to. My client was competent, had capacity, and did not have a problem with this. But I did!

I made sure to do my due diligence and screen out the possibility of financial exploitation. But no, Thomas was resigned to the fact that his son was a bit of malingerer and supported him. This was not one of the issues Thomas was "working on" in counseling either. *So why was I upset about it?*

Countertransference. I was having an emotional reaction to something going on with the client's life. Fortunately, I have had plenty of training on recognizing it and dealing with it. I talked to a colleague at the practice about why this was bothering me so much. It came down to the fact that my values didn't support this dynamic. For one, I was raised to work hard unless you can't. For another, in my family, younger people help out the elder loved ones, not the other way around.

No big deal. I resolved it by talking it through with a colleague and "managing" my countertransference. But what if I hadn't worked it through? What if I came to sessions with Thomas and berated him for not giving his son "tough love?" What if I opted to push my agenda onto Thomas when he was perfectly fine with his relationship with his son? That would have been a major problem. That would have led to some very unobjective, unethical practices.

Let's step away from shrink talk for a moment and step into a boating analogy. Being boaters, my husband Sean and I are popular in spring, summer, and fall. Friends and family flock to our bayfront town to join us on voyages throughout the Chesapeake Bay and its tributaries.

Sean is an excellent captain and is always very mindful about safety. He insists that we always give every guest the safety orientation, even if they've boated with us previously. We let passengers know where the life jackets, first aid kit, and other essentials are located. Life jackets are required for children under a certain age. But perhaps one of the most important announcements involves instructions about holding onto the railing when boarding and departing the vessel.

A couple years ago, we added a little story to the boating safety lesson. We let everyone know that my beautiful cousin Sarah had slipped and fallen into the water when she was disembarking. Everyone who knows Sarah was really startled by this story because Sarah is a registered yoga teacher! She is one of the most fit, flexible, agile people I have ever met. And when this fall happened, she was in her mid-twenties.

Now, Sarah *was* holding on to the railing when she fell into the water, but the mere fact that someone with such grace, balance, and flexibility could go into the drink illustrates the point that *anyone can fall in.*

The same goes for countertransference. Nobody is immune. Why? Because when you are a human being serving another human being, feelings are involved. Particularly in the intimate settings in which all of us lead and practice. If you never had any feelings about your clients, patients, or their family caregivers, you would be a robot. It doesn't matter if you have an MD, an MPH, and an MBA. It doesn't matter if you've been practicing medicine for forty years. If you are human, you will experience countertransference. Countertransference is normal. But Camaraderie Contagious leadership acknowledges it and makes accommodations for clinicians, paraprofessionals, and ancillary staff to process it. This is essential so patient care remains objective. But it is also essential so your employees are as psychologically healthy as possible.

So how does this play out when someone isn't a psychotherapist? Let's go back to Joe the chef and the senior living resident Ben. Joe had a lot in common with Ben. Ben even reminded Joe of his recently deceased uncle. Could there maybe be a version of countertransference occurring? Some of you may say no, Joe and Ben might just enjoy each other's company. But it is worth considering the possibility when a patient, client, or family caregiver is being treated differently than others by your employees.

It's important to remember that countertransference isn't actually the problem, though. It's when we don't manage it. Countertransference is really only well-managed when an employee feels safe discussing it and working out her feelings.

Dr. El-Aswad says it's an act of courage when an organization acknowledges that burnout is real. It's an even braver act to take action to prevent and tackle it. I believe if compassion fatigue and countertransference *and burnout* are acknowledged, prevented, and tackled too, a Contagious Camaraderie Culture is much more likely for the organization. In order to do this, you have to: create and reinforce whatever boundary policies are critical in your practice setting, encourage your team members to tell you what their boundaries are, and provide resources when they are struggling with burnout, compassion fatigue, and countertransference.

Want to do a quick check of your boundaries? Check out this quick Professional Boundary Assessment courtesy of my company, Jenerations Health Education Inc. Feel free to download a hard copy to share with your team at www.reimaginingcustomerserviceinhealthcare.

Jenerations Health Education, Inc.

www.jenerationshealth.com

Professional Boundary Assessment, Copyright 2009; Updated 2022.

How likely are you to do or have done the following:

(1) would never do it

(2) probably not do it

(3) possibly would do it

(4) highly likely do it

(5) always do it

1. ...given out my personal cell phone number to a client, patient, or family caregiver even if that is not my organization's standard protocol.
2. ...met socially with client, patient, or family caregiver outside of work hours to discuss my personal issues.
3. ...have given out my personal email address to a client, patient, or family caregiver if that is not my organization's standard protocol.
4. ...have connected with clients, patients, or family caregiver on social media.
5. ...date or consider dating or having a romantic/sexual relationship with a client, patient, or family caregiver.
6. ...do other freelance work outside of my job for a client, patient, or family caregiver without clearing it with my organization.
7. ...spent extra time with a client, patient, or family caregiver just because I like him or her.
8. ...disclose significant, detailed personal information with a client, patient, or family caregiver.
9. ...allow a client, patient, or family caregiver to monopolize my time when I have other work to do.
10. ...accept expensive gifts from clients, patients, or family caregivers.

11. ...dress differently when I will be spending time with a client, patient, or family caregiver I find attractive.
12. ...visit the client, patient, or family caregiver at home even if this is not my organization's standard protocol.
13. ...talk about my personal problems with a client, patient, or family caregiver because I think they would uniquely understand.
14. ...hire a client, patient, or family caregiver to do work for me or my family (housecleaning, babysitting, etc.).
15. ...expect reciprocity in the relationship with a client, patient, or family caregiver.
16. ...take things that the client, patient, or family caregiver does personally.
17. ...feel upset when the client, patient, or family caregiver does not show appreciation for my efforts.
18. ...allow the client, patient, or family caregiver to run our meetings.
19. ...buy expensive or frequent gifts for the client, patient, or family caregiver.
20. ...call or visit the client, patient, or family caregiver during my non-working hours.

Score

Add up the total number

0–20 Extremely Conservative Boundaries

21–40 Conservative Boundaries

41–60 Moderate Boundaries

61–80 Needs Help with Boundaries Very Soon

81–100 SOS! Needs Immediate Help Developing Boundaries

RECOGNITION: SHOW YOUR TEAM MEMBERS THEY ARE VALUED (DON'T JUST TELL THEM!)

As a professional speaker, coach and consultant who works with all kinds of healthcare, senior living, and mental health settings, I have access to a much deeper view of an organization's culture when I present at one of their internal meetings. I always try to attend the event early and stay late when my schedule allows so I can get a feel for the employees, the leadership, and their challenges and successes.

Several years ago, I was scheduled to speak at the internal sales and marketing meeting for Artis Senior Living. Artis Senior Living is a private-pay company that provides assisted living services to older adults and their families. They are very well known for their expertise in memory care—in particular, helping family caregivers transition their loved ones who have different types of dementia, including Alzheimer's disease, vascular, frontotemporal, and Lewy body. The company name "Artis" is actually an acronym that spells out their guiding principles for engaging with their residents, family caregivers, staff, and community partners: A—Ability to have a voice; R—Respecting and maintaining relationships; T—Treasuring each person's uniqueness; I—Integrity; S—Success and Recognition.

I had long been impressed with the culture and leadership of this organization. But when I walked into the conference center that day, I was almost moved to tears. Every salesperson had an assigned seat—and at that seat was a basket of snacks and treats. This was not just a generic basket, mind you. The national sales director, Andrea Marchesotti, and vice president of marketing, Amy DePreker, had taken the time to hand-select the favorite goodies of each individual salesperson. So if an employee loved Peppermint Patties, bananas, and Kind bars, that was at their seat. If another employee's favorite indulgence was double-stuffed Oreos, Gatorade, and peanut-butter crackers, that's what they found in their basket.

When I asked the leadership about these snacks and how on earth they came up with the idea, they said, "We wanted to do something for the 'T' in Artis." They were treasuring each person's uniqueness.

The snack baskets at the tables were personal. Individualized. Unexpected. And the team members felt special. All for an employee appreciation initiative that probably cost less than twenty dollars per person. Do you think that these team members felt valued and ready to provide the best possible service when they returned to their senior living communities? From witnessing it firsthand, I can tell you that they were. What can you do that is similar?

Cara Silletto, founder of Magnet Culture, believes that knowing your employees intimately and showing them that you understand their needs as individuals goes a long way toward creating a Contagious Camaraderie Culture. During the pandemic, her salesperson's husband was considered essential, so she was home by herself, trying to help her two elementary school-age children deal with distance learning. When Cara became aware of the problem, she offered to pay for childcare so her employee could continue to do her job. (This particular employee's job really needed to be done during business hours.) This money for childcare was *in addition* to her usual pay. Did Cara give every one of her team members extra cash during the pandemic? No, because not everyone had the issue her salesperson did. Cara has another employee who doesn't have kids but has several "fur babies." Cara built bereavement leave for when a pet dies into this employee's benefit package. What a beautiful example of *showing* team members they are valued rather than just *telling* them.

Demonstrating value for a team member is not only about doing something thoughtful at a team meeting or making individual accommodations. It also includes the daily small actions. For example, Dr. Anderson at Banner Health says, "There's not a day that goes by in my job that I don't check in with the staff." During the pandemic, when they lost several medical assistants, he checked in with the remaining team several times per day to ask, "How are you managing?" and "What support do you need?"

Alan Levin, DNP, MBA, RN, CPHQ, NEA-BC, vice president and chief nursing officer at NewYork-Presbyterian Queens Hospital, is a C-suite leader who has taken to social media to regularly recognize his employees. "We do an employee engagement satisfaction survey annually...and one of the questions asks, 'Have you been recognized in the last seven days?'"

Making sure all employees are acknowledged each week is a big undertaking in a large hospital such as Levin's! While Levin loves sending staff handwritten notes, he began embracing electronic thank-you notes so he can copy team members' bosses on the messages. But he has also found that social media shout-outs are one of the most efficient ways to praise the great work of his employees. He's even taught classes for other C-suite healthcare leaders on how to build momentum with this strategy. He finds that his clinicians tend to use Instagram, and leaders are more likely to utilize Twitter, so he tries to post on multiple platforms.

Some examples of Levin's posts (with photographs) include:

- recognizing the promotion of a nurse on Instagram. Not only did he congratulate this individual, but he mentioned that this gentleman spoke four languages

- acknowledging administrative staff for Administrative Professionals Day. In recognizing one administrative staff member, he mentioned how much she smiles at work

- praising the efforts of staff who got to their hospital shifts on an inclement weather day

How might these posts motivate the staff to put forth extra effort for their patients? I bet the nurse recognized for his promotion and language skills will be even more proud to interpret for patients and families. I'm guessing the administrative staff recognized for smiling will know that their positive facial expressions are making an impact on colleague and patient moods and will continue to smile. Those staff applauded for finding their way to the hospital during a snowstorm will probably be even more motivated to get to work when the weather's lousy. All of this contributes to the Contagious Camaraderie Culture, but it also is going to have a spin-off effect to the patients and their families.

"An engaged employee has that discretionary effort," says Levin. An engaged employee might bring in a brand of soap or tea that a patient likes, for example. In Bob Kelleher's YouTube video *Employee Engagement: Who's Sinking Your Boat*, Kelleher describes discretionary effort as "the above-and-beyond effort people could give if they wanted to."

Another great *show* rather than *tell* example of recognizing discretionary effort is Covenant Living's Inspired to Serve program. "Inspired to Serve gives all employees an opportunity to be recognized or to recognize others for following the services standards. Our residents and their family members are also able to participate in the recognitions when they see or experience great service. It's a recognition for a 'job well done.'" Terri Cunliffe, Covenant Living's president and CEO, goes on to say, "Supervisors are able to give rewards to employees who are going above and beyond. These rewards are then able to be redeemed at an online catalog, which has thousands of items ranging from gift cards, electronics, household items, and more."

Unfortunately, even if leaders regularly attempt to show their employees that they are valued, it can all be wiped out by a careless action. Let's say you are a regional manager for a large physical therapy company with locations all over the country. On a Friday afternoon, you and your colleagues nationwide receive this brisk email from your boss, Zach:

> ***Subject line:*** *regional manager opening at the San Diego office*
>
> *Hi Everyone,*
>
> *Since Ray is leaving, we now have another opening. Please let me know if you know of anyone for this location—as you know, we pay relocation costs.*

Well, you had no idea that Ray was leaving. You and Ray are friends and went through orientation together thirteen years ago. Within minutes of receiving the email from your boss, you get two texts and three emails from colleagues, asking if you know what's going on with Ray. Did Ray get fired? Is Ray okay?

You have no idea, so you pick up the phone and call him. Ray hasn't yet seen the email but explains that he simply gave notice because he was recruited by another physical therapy company for a job with more responsibility and better pay. Ray takes a look at the email and says, "Wow—seriously? Zach doesn't even say, 'let's wish

Ray good luck' or 'thanks for the last thirteen years' or anything like that. Kind of cold. But yeah, I'm excited about the new job!"

You congratulate Ray and promise to stay in touch. But when you reach out to the rest of your colleagues who were inquiring about Ray's departure, everyone is abuzz with disgust and disbelief. If Zach is that indifferent to a successful, thirteen-year employee departing the company, what about the rest of us? Are we all just disposable?

Most of the time, when an email like that goes out without any congratulations or accolades for the departing employee, everyone makes the assumption that something unpleasant has occurred, most likely a termination. Maybe Zach was just having a busy day when he shot off that curt email, but look at the impact it had on morale. Do you think those physical therapy regional managers were feeling great about their company that day? While questioning their value to the organization, do you think they provided the best possible service to patients that day?

Here's the good news. If you've done a lot of recognizing your employees, treating them with kindness, compassion, and empathy, if you make a gaffe like this, you are much more likely to be given the benefit of the doubt. Your employees will know you to be a thoughtful, caring leader and assume that you were just busy and distracted. But if your team does not have confidence in you as a caring leader, this type of blunder will cost you greatly in terms of your Contagious Camaraderie Culture. Making it right by sending a follow-up email congratulating Ray and owning up to your hasty message will also be restorative.

Let's discuss a few more ways to recognize your staff.

Want something free or very low cost?

Jeff Frum of Silverado says their communities have "gratitude trees." Employee and family members of residents can write short thank you "shout-outs" to employees they want to recognize.

Heather Guerieri of Compass says, "providing flexible schedules for working parents" has been very successful, as well as "writing stories about our staff and featuring them online for special months/weeks like Nurse's Week, Social Work Month, CNA Week." These stories are also often featured in the local newspapers.

George King, director of practice operations at For All Seasons Inc., a large mental health nonprofit in Maryland, says that their organization likes to "occasionally bring treats or cards or give shout-outs to recognize someone who goes above and beyond, as well as someone who does quality work day in and day out." King thinks it's important to acknowledge those who do quality work on a daily basis, so they don't feel taken for granted.

Janice Martin, founder of Senior Liaison of Central Florida Inc., a senior living placement service, has more than a decade of experience in assisted living sales and marketing. She describes a strategy that she found very motivating while working at an assisted living community. Every single morning, the expectation was that the entire staff would participate in a meeting from 9:10 to 9:20 a.m. Every community in the company did the same thing at the same time. Now, "stand-up" meetings are pretty standard in senior living and nursing home settings. But this was a bit different from other stand-up meetings Martin had experienced for two reasons: a motivational quote, tip, or concept was shared, and all employees—not just managers—attended unless they were directly providing care at that moment. Every single employee at every level in every department attended. This meeting was led by someone from the corporate office who was responsible for customer service training. Martin describes this as unifying as well as motivating because, "Everybody in the company—not just in the community I worked in, but every community they had—was doing the same thing every day at the same time. So we all had the same message that we were talking about." What a simple, innovative way to develop a sense of team across an organization.

Daniel Blum of Sinai Hospital and LifeBridge Health cites his organization's "You Asked, We Did" program. A team member makes a suggestion and you let them know you heard the suggestion by *showing*. For example, employees asked for chairs to be placed on the lawn of the hospital campus so they can eat outside at lunchtime on nice days. The staff at Sinai Hospital moved some chairs outside. Then, they highlighted that "You Asked, We Did" when they informed staff that they could dine al fresco on break.

Want to spend some money? Here are more some ideas!

Jeff Frum says that, particularly in California, their staff loves the In-N-Out food trucks they occasionally bring to their locations for employee recognition events.

John Dumas, USMC (Ret.), MBA, is the president and chief executive officer of Washington, DC-area nonprofit Service Coordination, which provides case management services to persons with developmental disabilities, and Montcordia, which provides upscale home care and care management services to ill persons in their homes. He says they reward their team members with outstanding benefits as well as "above industry-average pay." This "above-industry-average pay" strategy was initiated before the Great Resignation.

Heather Guerieri says they offer holiday parties, a robust PTO (personal time off) program, as well as team-building events with outside consultants.

Denise Manifold of Brightview Senior Living shared that during the early stages of the pandemic, when grocery shelves were bare, all their communities provided "pantries" to associates. Those working during that difficult time could get essentials (like toilet paper!) at the community free of charge.

ENCOURAGE STAFF INVOLVEMENT IN CUSTOMER SERVICE INITIATIVES

In many healthcare settings, "you have safety committees," says Janice Martin, founder of Senior Liaison. "Why not have a customer service committee?" She recommends that healthcare settings create hospitality committees from different departments. Doing this eliminates the feeling that the top executives are forcing service initiatives that are one more thing to do: "Oh, there they go again, another expectation on us."

DON'T EVEN THINK ABOUT LAUNCHING A CUSTOMER SERVICE INITIATIVE THAT YOU DON'T PLAN TO FOLLOW THROUGH ON

Martin describes working at a senior living company that presented a new program called Resident of the Month (program name changed to protect the identity of the organization) by the corporate office. The idea was that one resident would be chosen. Staff were to interview the resident, find out what their idea of a perfect day was, and then make that day happen. When she was told about the concept, Martin said, "I thought it was brilliant." But sadly, as long as she worked at this organization, leadership never made a plan to roll it out. She found herself "very disappointed" that such a cool idea was presented but never implemented.

DEMONSTRATE AUTHENTIC LEADERSHIP

In Jill Vitale-Aussem's book *Disrupting the Status Quo of Senior Living: A Mindshift*,[21] she describes an incredible leadership strategy. Although she's now the president and CEO of Christian Living Communities, she previously worked as an administrator of senior living communities. Vitale-Aussem would check herself into the community as a resident for a twenty-four-hour period.

She discusses what a humbling experience it was, wearing a lap buddy in a wheelchair and being seated at a "feeder" table and how difficult it was to sleep. She kept a diary of her experiences and says that after functioning as a temporary resident for only twenty-four hours, it took her two days to feel like herself again. Can you imagine working for a leader that would do this? Someone who literally put herself in the residents' bed?

There are going to be tough days at work! Even as you are striving for your staff to have a great experience and look forward to work. Leaders need to be genuine and authentic with their encouragement.

As Alan Levin says, "I tell staff, the goal is that you have more good days than bad days."

BE REALLY CAREFUL ABOUT GOING OVER AN EMPLOYEE'S HEAD

Sometimes it's necessary to go over an employee's head. Maybe there was a colossal mistake on the part of the employee. But sometimes you are going to go over their head in order to restore goodwill in the name of customer service. Just make sure that the employee saves face and you aren't undermining their authority.

AVOID A PURELY GERONTOCRATIC LEADERSHIP

In *Management Lessons from Mayo Clinic: Inside One of the World's Most Admired Service Organizations*,[22] authors Leonard L. Berry and Kent D. Seltman describe how Mayo Clinic's pay system does not incent leaders to remain in high-level positions indefinitely. There is not a pay cut to move out of leadership and back into a clinical role. This is brilliant. They are able to avoid burnout and the attitude of "that's the way we've always done it." That said, leaders who are thriving in their roles don't have to change positions if they don't want to. But having the option is empowering and contributes to a Contagious Camaraderie Culture.

CULTIVATE A CULTURE OF RESPECT FOR EVERYONE, NOT JUST LEADERS AND DOCTORS

Management Lessons from Mayo Clinic also emphasizes how important it is that everyone feel respected—not just physicians. Especially in traditional medical settings like hospitals, staff have been historically trained to defer to the physician. Physicians are considered the kings or queens of the medical profession. But physicians can't do their jobs without the teamwork and cooperation of every other department. When someone comes to work feeling that they are not as important as others in the organization, resentment breeds. And because staff cultures are contagious, you don't want that feeling going viral.

One of the reasons James Lee, co-founder of Bella Groves, created his own dementia education company is because he observed that many companies in the senior living industry would only promote after a certain period of time, even if a younger, less seasoned employee was a star. One of the goals for his company is to promote based on the value a team member brings to an organization rather than their age or length of service. He described the attitude that he encountered from some companies to be "cool your heels, kid." I have seen this concept play out a lot in healthcare, mental health, and senior living organizations. Promoting based on merit is much more effective.

COMMUNICATE YOUR EXPECTATIONS AND WISHES CLEARLY

I was an exceptional student—until about seventh grade. I was studying hard for a history test and was so stressed out that I told my parents I was going to skip my basketball game that night because I was scared I wasn't going to do well on the test. My father, Hank (you heard about his borderline traits in chapter 2), took my history book away and would not return it. He insisted that I go play at the basketball game. I was shocked and extremely upset. After we returned from the basketball game, I asked Hank for my book back and he refused. He said, "You either know it or you don't."

I don't remember how I did on that test. But I do remember that was the night I got the message that studying shouldn't be a priority anymore. I went through the rest of my school years until my freshman year of college being a very average student when I could have been much better if I'd actually studied. Around my sophomore year of college, I had an epiphany that it was *my* life; I was an adult, and I could study as much as I wanted to.

I'm not saying that turning me off from academics was my father's intention. In fact, he was pretty pissed when I brought home report cards with Bs, Cs, and the occasional D. But I was confused; what did my parents want from me? Looking back on the situation as an adult, I know I could have handled it differently. Maybe I could have had a conversation with my dad about expectations. Unfortunately, I didn't have the emotional maturity to do that. And because of my dad's mental health issues, it may not have been helpful if I did.

Confusion about expectations happens a lot in health and mental health workplaces, especially since they are so busy. While leaders are going to give mixed messages sometimes, it's important to try to be as consistent as possible when discussing priorities, helping staff interpret mission and goals, and to have an open door when team members need clarification.

Be clear about what's happening and what's expected from your employees. Daniel Blum believes that multimodal communication to team members throughout the enterprise is crucial. He says his leaders rely on a blend of town hall meetings, unit-based rounding, cascading messages, and role-modeling behavior. If you know something is coming up that will impact team members, whether positive or negative, communicate those messages early.

Rick Evans, senior vice president and chief experience officer for NewYork-Presbyterian Hospital, says that patient engagement and satisfaction is a high priority within their entire healthcare system. Team members are evaluated on their performance, and they are aware of it well ahead of time. Not only are the expectations clearly spelled out, Evans and his department provide evidence-based ideas for how to achieve success in patient engagement.

PUT YOUR MONEY WHERE YOUR MOUTH IS

I almost didn't include this piece of advice because I know there are small organizations for whom this section, if fully implemented, might put them out of business. But there are a lot of people reading this who can throw some money at creating a more Contagious Camaraderie Culture, so I decided to include it.

Yes, recognizing your employees is important. In fact, there are studies that indicate many employees find having a good boss and being recognized are even more important than their financial compensation. But compensation is still important. And as we've discussed, health, mental health, and senior living employees have a lot of choices. Particularly those who are not clinicians! So money does matter.

Terri Cunliffe, the president and CEO of Covenant Living, says, "the shrinking labor pool was impacting everyone. We reviewed our wages and benefits, and for those in healthcare, we made wage adjustments to remain competitive in the market. It was one way we could make an impact on retaining those who've already made relationships with our residents and their family members. We've really been pushing our Employee Referral program to bring in additional new-hire prospects. All employees can refer friends, family, or anyone they know who might be a good fit within the organization. If the individual is hired and stays on the job, that referring employee is given a referral bonus ranging from two hundred to five thousand dollars depending on the position filled."

According to Cara Silletto, founder of Magnet Culture, Covenant Living's strategy is right on target. "The organizations who are hyper-aware that current workloads have become unsustainable--they're proactively working to prune jobs back down to a manageable level. They're reworking budgets and profit margin expectations for the long haul," she says.

For those of you who can't boost salaries and other benefits, it's critical to work extra hard on the other strategies we discussed in this chapter. For those of you who can, think about how much more desirable your workplace will be if you are able to integrate both!

CHAPTER 8
What Influences the Client/Patient Experience

CLIENT KARMA

We talked about Team Karma in the last chapter. As we discussed, when we have built up enough Team Karma, our team members are much more likely to be loyal and stay with us longer. They are also more likely to provide fantastic service to our patients, clients, and family caregivers.

Client Karma is the concept that building up goodwill is the key to getting our patients, clients, and family caregivers to trust us more and be happier with our services. They are more likely to give us positive reviews and less likely to complain and/or sue. Most importantly, like employees who have experienced Team Karma, these customers will give you the benefit of the doubt when there is a perceived slight, inconvenience, or disappointment in service. When we consistently treat our patients, clients, and family caregivers with respect, compassion, and empathy, we are typically rewarded with the benefits of Client Karma.

As I was writing this book, I came across a tweet that basically sums up this entire chapter. On April 2, 2022, Janice Dean, meteorologist and *New York Times* bestselling author of *Mostly Sunny* and *Make Your Own Sunshine*,[23] tweeted, "I went to get blood work done this morning and fasted yesterday. The nurse that drew my blood wasn't very nice. I feel like that's a job where you have to be nice to people." Indeed, Janice.

Of course, patients, clients, and their families want great clinical outcomes, but they also just hope you will be nice to them, as Janice indicated in her tweet.

Every interaction with any customer in any setting has the potential to increase or decrease stress. Every single interaction! You may be thinking, *Does the concept of Client Karma really apply to a quick visit to get blood drawn?* Absolutely it does. And you can tell that this blood draw location did not create Client Karma. Why? Because of Ms. Dean's tweet!

Let's step out of healthcare and into retail for a moment to illustrate this point. Years ago, I walked into my favorite department store. I'll call it "Lacy's." This was after a long but uneventful day at work. I began walking around the ladies' section browsing the suits, dresses, and other professional clothing. Thankfully, this was not a shopping trip with a true agenda like needing an outfit for a specific event. I just decided to see if there was anything I liked that could supplement my work wardrobe for keynotes and coaching meetings.

I began to pick up suits, dresses, blouses, and slacks. As I gathered items into my arms, I walked by the cash register area where two female employees were chatting. I kept walking around the store for another twenty minutes or so until my arms could carry no more and finally decided to brave the fitting room with all the other women trying on clothes.

I don't know if you've ever "been there," but the fitting room was not a fun place for me that evening. Nothing looked good. I had a little PMS and was probably bloated. I silently cursed the cheesesteaks and soft pretzels I'd eaten when I was back in my hometown of Philly the previous weekend.

Suddenly, I heard a loud, take-charge voice in the fitting room say, "Ladies!" I immediately thought, *Oh good! Someone is here who is going to offer help. Maybe some of these clothes will look nicer if I get a bigger size.* But the voice did not offer help. It went on to say, "If you aren't purchasing the items you are trying on, we're going to need you to hang them up on the rack outside the dressing room." I poked my head out of my room and saw that it was one of the clerks I'd seen earlier chatting by the register.

On a scale of zero to ten (zero being feeling no stress and ten being maximum stress), I went from a three to a seven in an instant. Well, it felt like an instant, but it really wasn't. Let's examine why I became so stressed out in that moment.

I walked in with my stress level at about a three. I wasn't under any pressure to buy clothes. I hadn't had a particularly stressful day before I entered the store.

What were the interactions that raised my stress level?

1. Walking by two employees who were chatting with each other and neither acknowledged me. No hello. No smile. Stress level rises to four without my realizing it

2. The clothes were getting heavy in my arms. The two employees who were *not* assisting other customers did not offer to help carry the clothes nor did they offer to open a fitting room for me. Stress level rises to five without my realizing it

3. It does not go well in the fitting room. Whether we want to blame the Philadelphia treats or PMS bloating, we can't put this one on the employees. But now my stress level is at six

4. The store clerk not only doesn't offer help with getting the proper sizes, she's putting me to work! Stress level is at seven

I was irritated enough to find a store manager and let her know how disappointed I was by the experience at Lacy's. I wound up leaving without purchasing anything. And really, who cares? It's not like I *needed* to buy something that night. But Lacy's missed out. Imagine the sales they might have made if the clerks had been given some BANWTH (boring advice nobody wants to hear—more on that shortly).

But never mind sales that evening. I think everyone who is reading this book knows the real name of the department store rhymes with "Lacy's." In addition to writing about it in this book, do you have any idea how many times I have told this story at an event? A lot.

If the clerks had built up even a little bit of Client Karma with me, I bet my stress level would not have risen to seven. Can you think of just one thing they could have done that might have prevented me from sharing my disappointment with the store manager?

Smile? Say hello? Ask if I needed a fitting room? Insist on carrying some items for me? Offer to get me a different size when I was in the fitting room? Ideally, all of that should have happened, but even *one* of them would have reduced my stress and built some Client Karma. If any one of those minor differences had occurred, I probably would not be telling this story so many years later.

How many times a day does a story like this play out in a healthcare setting? Countless. But the stakes are far higher—often life and death. Of course, healthcare customers are always dealing with more stress than the average customer shopping for clothes. On a scale of zero to ten, their stress level is typically over seven when they have their first interaction with your organization. As we discussed in chapter 1, they are SOA! Stressed on arrival! Let's take a look at an example.

Aidan and his wife, Sue, have been caring for his dad, Bill, for the last several years at home. Bill has advanced Parkinson's disease dementia. They have come to the conclusion that they just can't keep Bill at home anymore. Aidan made a list of assisted living communities in their area. He calls the first one on the list and nobody answers the phone. He calls a second time, and the receptionist puts him on hold immediately. When she returns to the line, the receptionist says, "You are calling about Mrs. Sawyer's medication, right?" "No," Aidan says, "I wanted to get information about your community." "Okay, who are you holding for?" the receptionist says. Aidan responds that he doesn't know. "It's fine—I will call back another time," he says and hangs up. But of course, Aidan never calls back. If the receptionist there can't be helpful or friendly when he calls to inquire about their services, there's no way it's the right place for his father.

Aidan's stress level was at about nine when he placed that first call. He and his wife had a tearful conversation the night before about placing his father in a community. Aidan's brother completely disagrees with the decision and is trying to persuade him to keep taking care of their father at home.

This first and only interaction with the community raised his stress tremendously. He got up to ten when nobody answered the phone the first time he called, eleven when he was put on hold, and twelve when the receptionist broke confidentiality and said the name of one of their residents.

What if Aidan's first call attempt had been answered on the second ring? And what if the receptionist had said, "May I please put you on a brief hold?" rather than putting him on hold automatically. How about if the receptionist had come back and said, "May I ask whom you are holding for?" if she was confused rather than talking about Mrs. Sawyer's medication. Then she might have had the opportunity to answer Aidan's question. With these small changes to the interaction, Aidan's stress level would likely have stayed the same or gone down to eight or seven rather than increasing.

THE HISTORY OF THE PATIENT AND CLIENT EXPERIENCE

Daniel Blum of Sinai Hospital and LifeBridge has been a lifelong advocate for better patient experiences. When he began his career in the 1980s, he found that, "Basically, it was a paternalistic system." The attitude back then of many healthcare leaders and clinicians used to be, "This is not Burger King. It's not 'have it your way'; you will have it my way because I'm the care provider, and you're the patient." Since then, Blum has been on a journey to transform that attitude in the healthcare systems he's led.

Chad Brough of Home Instead agrees with this perspective, based on his past experiences in hospital settings. He suggests that home care organizations, for example, have to be different because they are a "consumer-facing business." He goes on to say, "One of the reasons healthcare is so broken is that healthcare has not traditionally been a consumer-based service. The referrals, the relationships come through payers.... That particular dynamic doesn't really push organizations to do what they should be doing for service delivery."

So how do we do this? How do we build Client Karma in health, mental health, and senior living?

DEVELOP RELATIONSHIPS BEFORE THERE'S A PROBLEM

Kevin Goedeke of Erickson Senior Living and NHA Stand-Up (whom we met in chapter 7), talked about how he considers his customers to include employees, residents, and residents' family members. Since you don't always see family members as often as residents and employees, he "learned early on that you have to be really intentional about how you communicate and build relationships with the family members."

He believes that healthcare leaders need to "be proactive and invest in having dialogue and communication...when you don't really have an agenda." If you are only talking to them about solving problems that they bring up before you've developed a rapport, you're at a disadvantage. "Your first two to three interactions and conversations should be for no reason at all, other than just wanting to get to know that person." This is an excellent example of *showing*, not just *telling*, that you care. At Erickson Senior Living, their Continuing Care Connection program assigns a leader to each new resident and their family members. "Their job is to reach out proactively" and develop a relationship with the new resident and their family through updates. If something is not quite right and the resident or family needs something, they already have a relationship with a staff person who has done friendly outreach prior to a concern occurring. He finds that this strategy succeeds in "depositing goodwill into that relationship." A perfect example of developing solid Client Karma!

BANWTH FOR BUILDING CLIENT KARMA

Let's take a look at one of my favorite topics: BANWTH (Boring Advice Nobody Wants to Hear). In my first book, *Cruising Through Caregiving: Reducing the Stress of Caring for Your Loved One*, I talk about how family caregivers can prepare for their own aging experience, so it goes as well as possible. People who have been family caregivers often want to minimize the chance that they will need a caregiver someday. I call those tips BANWTH. And of course, as a healthcare leader or staff member, I am sure you all know what BANWTH for them was:

- Eat healthfully
- Moderate caffeine and alcohol
- Get a good night's sleep
- Reduce stress
- Maintain strong social connections

- Exercise
- Get routine medical and dental care

Blah, blah, blah.

Look, I know people hate hearing about BANWTH from *Cruising Through Caregiving* because (almost) everyone already knows it. But BANWTH is the stuff (almost) everyone knows but not everyone is doing. It's common sense. It's obvious. It "should" come naturally for everyone. *But it doesn't!* If it did, most people would be 100 percent physically, mentally, and cognitively healthy, but they aren't. People struggle to get enough sleep. They eat junk food and drink too much alcohol. They don't exercise. They are stressed out all the time and not relaxing enough. But while most people know what will help them, they find the advice tedious. They want to hear something new and exciting, like a Vitamin X was invented that guarantees perfect mental, physical, and cognitive health. But we all know that eating healthfully, moderating alcohol, exercising, sleeping well, reducing stress, and getting preventive care are all the keys to the best possible health.

What's some super obvious advice that make up the basic tenets of Client Karma? No matter what practice setting you are in, they are the same. Whether you are an auto repair shop, a grocery store, a restaurant, or a doctor's office, the BANWTH is the same. Hint: we talked about this a little while ago at the end of the Lacy's story. Take a moment and write one or two down before reading any further.

Did you write down "Smile"? You'd be right.

Did you write down "Say hello when you see a patient or client in the hallway"? Yep.

How about asking a waiting patient or client, "Have you been helped?" or "How many I assist you?" Yes!

Did you write down "Nodding"? That's one too!

What about "Make eye contact"? Check.

A quick acronym that can help you remember is SHANE (named after my favorite character on *The L Word* and its reboot,

The L Word: Generation Q). Shane is played by the beautiful and talented actor Katherine Moennig. Incidentally, Shane exhibits all of the BANWTH in her fictional careers as both a hair stylist and a bar owner. For those of you who aren't familiar with *The L Word*, perhaps you'd rather remember it by thinking of the Irish meaning of the word: *God is gracious*.

- S—Smile
- H—Hello
- A—Ask if they need help
- N—Nod
- E—Eye Contact

They're all really simple. And they're all the small things that the staff at Lacy's didn't do during my visit. I'm guessing not everyone at your workplace is practicing SHANE all the time. If they were, you'd have far fewer complaints or poor reviews. When leaders ask me to help their teams do better with service and patient engagement, I begin to talk about these SHANE basics, and they look dumbfounded. "It can't be that simple. My people know better," they say. Many of them may know better, but it doesn't mean they are practicing SHANE every day. It's not rocket science. But by embracing SHANE, you incorporate an important line of defense for preventing problems and ultimately transforming patients, clients, and family caregivers from "hateful" to "grateful."

While the BANWTH principles are the same for customer service across the board, we know the stakes for health, mental health, and senior living are far higher than they are at Lacy's, the grocery store, the auto repair shop, or a restaurant. Far higher. As we discussed in earlier chapters, we health, mental health, and senior living providers are seeing people at their most stressed and most vulnerable. The BANWTH counts in our practice settings more than we can imagine.

Can you honestly say that everyone who works for your organization is smiling, saying hello, making eye contact, and asking to help each and every patient, client, and family caregiver they encounter? If not, don't worry! While we are going to discuss more helpful customer service and patient engagement strategies throughout this chapter, we are going to discuss how to get your team to actually do them in the next one.

Besides SHANE, what else is going to help your team transform patients, clients, and family caregivers from "hateful" to "grateful" and create Client Karma?

1. Treat prospective healthcare customers like they are already your customers.

Denise Manifold of Brightview Senior Living shared that their teams strive to help anyone who may call upon them for guidance. "Even if we're talking to someone who may not ever move into our community or refer to our community, we still want to help them," she says. I can tell you firsthand that this is absolutely true. I have called upon associates at different Brightview locations numerous times over the years to ask for referrals for elder law attorneys, home care agencies, and support groups for friends and family who are looking for assistance. Every time I have done this, I have been treated professionally and politely and the associates have gone out of their way to guide me. Does this make me want to suggest Brightview if someone I know is looking in an area where they provide services? Of course!

2. Avoid inflammatory language.

Terms like "short-staffed" incite fear and stress in your patients and clients. Even if you are short-staffed, be careful about saying so. Try to find other language that does not conjure up the image of a nearly empty hospital with one nurse treating fifty patients. Maybe something like, "Please accept our apologies for the wait. We are waiting on another occupational therapist to arrive before you can be seen."

3. *Be careful about using abbreviations and acronyms.*

Avoid saying and writing acronyms and abbreviations that are not common knowledge. Sure, there are probably plenty of people who understand that "UTI" means "urinary tract infection," but many do not. ADL (activities of daily living), CXL (cancelled), SA (suicide attempt), and f/u (follow up) are among just a few of the many abbreviations that can be confusing. Many of us don't even realize we are doing it.

I'm going to assume that most readers are not computer technology experts. But think about when a technology expert is trying to help you solve a problem and they start using words you don't understand. That person is probably not trying to "talk over your head," but when they start using that jargon, it makes an already stressful situation (internet out!) more difficult. And to be fair, the internet going out isn't in the same ballpark as having a serious health or mental health problem.

4. *Consider the way you word communication.*

Once, on vacation at a very upscale resort, my husband and I spent the day at their beach club. When the sun started to go down—our favorite time of day—the staff began going around and alerting the dozens of guests who were still enjoying the beach that they had to leave. Unpleasantly surprised by this, I found a manager to clarify what time the beach club closed, and he said, "Yes, this is about the time we kick people out." Wow! Talk about a poor choice of words.

"No problem" is another one of my least favorite idioms. When I go to a restaurant and ask for more water and am told, "No problem," even if it's with a smile, I think, *Could it have been a problem?* or *Would there ever be a time where such a request has been a problem?* Why would anyone want to ever put a negative term like "problem" in a customer's mind unless there is no other option?

Another time when we commonly hear "no problem" is when someone says "Thank you." I have actually said "Thank you" when receiving change from a cashier and have heard "No problem." What ever happened to "You're welcome?"

"My pleasure" is the response you will get from well-trained employees at the Ritz-Carlton and Chick-fil-A when you ask for something.

Other good responses to a client or patient request instead of "no problem" may include:

- "Glad to take care of that."
- "Happy to help you."
- "Let me get that for you."
- "I'll be right back with that."
- "Let me check to see if we can get that for you."
- "I'm so sorry we don't have that available. Is there something else we might get for you?"

Other good responses to a client or patient saying "thank you" may include:

- "You're welcome."
- "Of course."
- "Thank *you* for your business today."
- "Glad to help. Have a great day!"

Beyond "no problem," there are other phrases that you likely want to avoid at your practice setting. For example, in Dee Ann Turner's book, *It's My Pleasure: The Impact of Extraordinary Talent and a Compelling Culture,*[24] she shares that Four Seasons

Hotel staff don't say that they are "sold out" when they have no rooms left. They respond that they are "fully committed."

Dr. Kamal from the American Cancer Society and Duke University says "words matter," particularly when discussing serious clinical diagnoses and treatments. During our interview, he shared the story of a patient who echoed back a conversation that they'd had ten years prior! He described this experience as humbling. Dr. Kamal believes that healthcare providers need to remember that patients "will likely remember most of what you say," particularly if the message is unexpected or one that elicits strong emotion. In chapter 7, he shared that sometimes healthcare providers assume that patients know how much they care. Dr. Kamal believes that just taking a few seconds to say, "I'm on your side and I'm here to support you" can make an enormous difference for the patient's state of mind. A beautiful moment like that positively impacts not just clinical outcomes but patient satisfaction as well.

5. Apologize.

Look—if you are chief medical officer at a hospital and one of your surgeons accidently amputated the wrong limb, you need to consult with your legal team on how to structure the conversation and apology. So let's table those kinds of apologies for a moment. I'm talking about the basic courtesy of apologizing for minor slights and wrongs that we are all involved in daily.

Juliet, the receptionist at the Seaside Chiropractic Office, forgot to call Mrs. Rose to cancel her appointment. The appointment needed to be rescheduled because the chiropractor's daughter was injured at a soccer game. Mrs. Rose came to the office in pain, eager to see the doctor. Juliet saw Mrs. Rose walk in, barely looked up from her desk, and said, "I see you didn't get my message." She then informed the patient that her appointment had been cancelled. Mrs. Rose checked her cell phone and confirmed that no message had been left. Juliet said, "Oh well, there must be something going on with your phone because I called all of the patients to let them know about the doctor's emergency. When would you like to reschedule?" No apology. How do you think Mrs. Rose responded to this?

As we've discussed repeatedly, no patient is excited to visit a doctor's office. Add the fact that Mrs. Rose is in pain. Combine that with Juliet's abrupt demeanor and lack of apology. On top of that, Juliet engages in "blaming" the patient's phone for the mistake.

This scenario plays out every single day, in every single industry. But in healthcare and mental health, as we've discussed, the stakes are much higher than at your local grocery store.

Of course, you probably guessed that Mrs. Rose was irate. Not only did she drive over to Seaside Chiropractic in traffic, in pain, she was now being blamed for the goof by the receptionist.

What if Juliet nodded empathically and simply said, "I'm so sorry. I really thought I'd left a message for you. I can't imagine how frustrated you are." How do you think Mrs. Rose would have responded? She still would've been upset, but I guarantee she would've been de-escalated—even if she happened to be one of the practice's "Always Difficult" patients.

Why would Juliet not simply apologize? I'm going to guess that she was never trained that apologizing for small mistakes is a small, simple way to de-escalate an upset client or patient. More on this in chapter 10.

6. Practice service recovery.

Peggy Funk is the executive director at Hospice & Palliative Care Network of Maryland and the former associate director of the Maryland Pharmacists Association. But before joining the healthcare field, she enjoyed a successful career in retail management, marketing, and public relations. She suggests that when healthcare providers make a mistake, they emulate what's common in retail: service recovery. For example, when a store customer would complain that a clerk was rude, they were often offered a gift card as a gesture of compensation.

What is the version of this that you can offer in your practice setting? In some settings, maybe you can give a gift card to your cafeteria or gift shop. Or, have some gift bags on hand with branded mugs and herbal tea or hot chocolate that you can give out on such occasions. Maybe mail a ten-dollar Amazon gift card with an apology note. Even just an apology email may be enough service recovery in some cases. If you are a dermatology office, perhaps you could offer a bag of your very best skin care product samples.

7. Limit how much they need to repeat.

In *An Epidemic of Empathy in Healthcare*, Dr. Thomas H. Lee discusses how exhausting and frustrating it is for a patient to be asked the same questions repeatedly. It's best practice for health, mental health, and senior living professionals to do the best they can to be prepared for meetings with their patients, clients, and caregivers. Review their chart or paperwork beforehand. Try to get caught up so you can ask good, clarifying questions rather than making the person start from scratch. Not only is it tiring to have to answer the same questions, it also causes the patient to worry that we don't know what we are doing.

8. Ask better questions.

Speaking of questions...Are you asking questions that make sense, or are you reading off of some screen or form like a robot? I went to an urgent care facility once because I had an annoying, lingering cough after a bad winter cold. My goal was to see if a provider thought there was a bacterial infection and if an antibiotic would help. (It seems like the answer is always no, but I thought I'd check.) The nurse practitioner who knew my presenting problem asked me, "On a scale of one to ten, how much pain do you have?" *Huh? I'm here for a cough*. There was no *pain*, thankfully. I just wanted the cough to go away. It definitely made me reluctant to go back to that urgent care center.

9. Be a human being when there's a serious mistake.

Earlier in the book, we talked about how Sorrel King lost her eighteen-month-old daughter, Josie, at Johns Hopkins Hospital due to a series of errors. Clearly, this is one of the most horrific mistakes that a healthcare institution can make. But how Johns Hopkins responded is a lesson in how to handle a serious, fatal mistake. Leadership apologized. They investigated how and why the mistakes happened. They communicated the details of that investigation to the family. Eventually, they partnered with the King family to bring patient safety programs to hospitals.

Nothing was ever going to bring Josie King back. But the fact that hospital leadership behaved like human beings rather than robots says a lot. Clearly, apologizing and attempting to compensate a patient's family for a mistake of this magnitude is going to require coördination and consults with financial and legal counsels. But for heaven's sake, don't make things worse by being sketchy. In fact, some data suggests that doing so increases the likelihood for lawsuits. For more information on the whole story, be sure to check out the book *Josie's Story*.

10. Have policies but know when to make exceptions.

Policies at your organization are important. Many of them, like keeping the fire door closed, always need to be followed. Some of them are more flexible (or should be) in the name of improving the customer experience.

While customer service author and expert David Avrin recognizes that sometimes the answer to a customer question really does have to be a "no," he makes a strong case for occasional exceptions. In his book *Why Customers Leave (and How to Win Them Back)*,[25] Avrin balks at the idea that if an exception is ever made for one customer that it would have to be made for everyone. I know just what he means.

For years, our family was a regular customer at our favorite bakery. We were friendly with the owner and staff and spent at a lot of money there each year. It was our go-to place for desserts when we had parties (several times per year) and for morning baked goods when we had friends and family overnight from out of town, and we even patronized them regularly for work events.

One day, I was cleaning out a drawer and found a misplaced gift card for the bakery. I put it in my purse and was excited to use it the next time I was in the shop. I didn't realize the gift card had expired. The clerk at the register said I wouldn't be able to use it. I asked if I could talk to the owner for a moment. The owner, whom we'd known for many years, told me that they would not honor the gift card. I said it had expired only recently and that I'd really appreciate if she'd redeem it since I was such a good customer. She responded that if she let me use it, she would have to do it for everyone.

No, she wouldn't. First of all, how many people are entering that bakery with an expired gift card? I doubt many, so it's unlikely she'd have to honor an endless number of recently expired gift cards. Second, the owner could choose to be flexible on this policy for a *regular customer*.

That bakery owner demolished a long-term, hard-won customer relationship over twenty dollars. And while I'm not one to trash any business on social media, I have told several people about that disappointing experience. Look—I get that the owner had every right to decline my request. But I also have every right to redirect my hard-earned dollars elsewhere.

What rules and policies are sacrosanct at your organization and which ones can be bent for people you know? How would you respond to a patient or client asking you to break these rules? Do you know how your team would respond?

- Amy, a psychotherapy client doesn't show up for her weekly appointment. She doesn't call to cancel. Your receptionist sends a "no-show" invoice. Several weeks later, Amy calls to apologize, letting you know that she got the bill, and the reason she didn't call to cancel is because her mother was rushed to the hospital. Amy has never "no-showed" before. Do you waive the fee?

- Bob is at your dental office getting his biannual teeth cleaning. He asks your hygienist if he could have an extra toothbrush in his complimentary "goodie bag" because he realizes he needs a new one for his travel bag. Do you give him a free extra toothbrush?

- Your pharmacy's cash register and computer system are down. A patient tells you she has no cash, but she's on the last day of her arthritis medication so she really needs the refill. She asks if perhaps you could give her a few pills and she can come back with her credit card later. Do you provide a partial refill?

I hope the answer to all of these vignettes is not a definitive "no." If you have a "hateful" to "grateful" mindset in your organization, you are at least considering making the exceptions the patients requested. And most of the time, I hope you do.

Organizations known for good customer service not only make these small, occasional exceptions, but they also are notorious for empowering their staff to do so. For example, Joseph A. Michelli's book *The Starbucks Experience: 5 Principles for Turning Ordinary Into Extraordinary*[26] details that baristas have the authority to give a free beverage to customers who have spilled their first one. Michelli's book about the Ritz-Carlton, *The New Gold Standard: 5 Leadership Principles for Creating Legendary Customer Experience Courtesy of The Ritz-Carlton Hotel Company*,[27] explains that all hotel employees are empowered to spend up to two thousand dollars per guest (without managerial approval) for service recovery issues. Peggy Funk of Hospice & Palliative Care Network of Maryland says that healthcare organizations need to embrace this same strategy of empowering their staff to fix problems: stop making them always get a manager to help the patient, client, or family caregiver.

The Mayo Clinic's version of this involves empowering staff in another way. They are strongly encouraged to pull in staff and resources from other departments if they don't believe the patient's needs are being met, according to *Management Lessons from Mayo Clinic.*

11. *Keep confidential information confidential.*

How many times have you heard or seen private healthcare information you were not entitled to see or hear? I have seen and heard countless pieces of confidential information not meant for my eyes and ears during my decades in health, mental health, and senior living. Yes, mistakes happen. But one of the quickest ways to lose the trust of patients and clients is for them to question whether or not their information is being kept private. The example of Aidan calling the assisted living facility earlier in this chapter is a great example.

A great way to *show* this rather than just *tell* is to have signs up in your office or facility that remind staff and others to be mindful of confidential information. More on this in chapter 11.

12. *Introduce yourself.*

As a patient or client, how many times have you interacted with persons from the healthcare system who never introduced themselves? I've had this experience countless times. For the love of God, servers at restaurants introduce themselves! The fact that this is not commonplace in health or mental health is absolutely appalling. We health and mental health professionals (and all ancillary staff) will come to know all kinds of intimate information and *see* all kinds of private parts. This is a simple way to build rapport with the patient or client and reduce nervousness. It's also just good manners.

13. Ask adult patients and clients how they would like to be addressed.

Not only is this another courtesy, but it can offer you *a lot* of insight about the person you are going to be treating. If a patient asks you to address her as Mrs. Wells, you know she is likely more conventional than someone who says, "Call me Val." When a patient says she'd like to be called Sister Mary Katherine, you have learned something important about who she is.

14. Don't make assumptions.

I'm going to take us out of healthcare for a moment to share one of my favorite personal stories about making assumptions. Several years ago, we went to Italy with a bunch of friends. They'd been there for a few days before we arrived. Sean and I were on such a high when we arrived that we wound up staying up really late, talking with everyone excitedly about all the fun we were going to have over the next week. Finally, we went to bed and slept like the dead. I woke up and looked at my phone and saw that the time was 2:45 p.m. I gasped and shook Sean awake. When I told him what time it was, he said "No way, you're looking at a different time zone." Sure enough, it was 2:45 p.m. CET. We looked at each other and started laughing.

Now here's the part about assumptions. Our dear friend Frank, who coordinated the trip, had been stressing all day that they didn't do enough to try to wake us up. They'd called, texted, and knocked gently on our door before setting off on the day's excursion. Poor Frank even seemed worried that we'd be mad at them. It sucked to lose most of our first day in Italy, but Sean and I actually thought it was very "us." We are known to sleep in on vacation.

Assuming did Frank no good that day. And it never does health or mental health professionals any good either.

Ed has been married to his husband, Patrick, for ten years. During his annual physical, Ed's physician, Dr. Reed, suggests an HIV test along with the rest of his routine blood work.

Lauren also has been married for ten years—to her husband, Ken. When she goes to Dr. Reed for her annual physical, an HIV test is not suggested.

Dr. Reed has made the assumption that Ed and Patrick are not monogamous and that Lauren and Ken are, which is blatantly homophobic. What he doesn't know is that Ed and Patrick are completely faithful. On the other hand, Lauren and Ken have an open marriage. Instead of taking the time to understand the type of risk factors that each of his patients faces, Dr. Reed jumped to the conclusion that a gay man and his husband must be sleeping around. He also assumed that a heterosexual couple were in a traditional marriage.

It would be one thing if Dr. Reed told his patients that he offers everyone an HIV test. But the strategy of relying on assumptions not only offended Ed but it left Lauren in an awkward spot of not feeling like she had the option when she wanted it. After all, people who are in nontraditional marriages are not always forthcoming because of fear of judgment.

In Joseph Michelli's book *The New Gold Standard* about the Ritz-Carlton, he emphasizes how the company strives not to make assumptions about what a guest would like. For example, staff are not to pour a beer into a glass if the guest prefers to drink it right out of the bottle. While many staff at a fine hotel, bar, or restaurant would automatically pour the beverage into a glass, the Ritz-Carlton staff are mindful that not everyone wants that.

How can you emulate what the Ritz-Carlton does with the beer by leaving room for the idea that your customer might want something different than you are expecting?

Let's say that in an effort to provide great service, your eye care office offers free overnight shipping of products to patients' homes. Your receptionist calls your patient Tony and says that his contact lenses are in and will be shipped. Tony responds that he'd prefer to pick them up at your office. Your earnest receptionist insists that he shouldn't have to make the twenty-minute trip and they will be shipped. The patient is then put in the embarrassing situation of saying that he is separated from his spouse and is not currently living at the address on file. It's great to offer options, but it's crucial to *listen* when patients, clients, and family caregivers are firm about what they want.

15. Let Your Patients, Clients, and Family Caregivers Know What to Expect.

Let's say you book a vacation at a beautiful waterfront hotel on the beach after a long year of hard work. You specifically pay extra for an ocean-view suite so you and your spouse can soak up the sunrise every morning from your private balcony before the kids wake up. Imagine your reaction when you go outside with your coffee to see and hear cranes, dump trucks, and construction workers. Another resort is being built next door. Most people would not be too happy about this noisy eyesore when they were expecting a serene view.

Do you think that this would have bothered you as much if the hotel had given you a heads-up? Maybe if they had a statement on their website and on the confirmation email that informed you about the construction? Or even if they mentioned it at check-in? Most people wouldn't like it, but they would appreciate knowing about the disruption ahead of time.

People don't like to be unpleasantly surprised on vacation, and they sure as hell don't like it when it comes to their healthcare. Consider when Rosanne went in for a hysterectomy. Terry from her surgeon's office called the day before to let her know she'd be spending one night in the hospital. While this was not what Rosanne and her doctor had discussed previously, Rosanne worked to wrap her mind around the change. *Okay, that makes sense—it's major surgery. They probably just want to watch me overnight to make sure everything is okay. It is probably much safer that way*, she thought. Rosanne packed a bag with a change of clothes, some magazines, and her toiletries. When Rosanne and her husband arrived at the hospital the next day, her surgeon smiled and nodded toward her bag, asking "Are you planning to move in?" Rosanne responded, "I'm staying over, right? That's what Terry said." The doctor shook his head and said that he would never keep her overnight unless there were serious complications. He likes to get his patients out of the hospital as quickly as is safe to avoid the possibility of an infection. Rosanne was already nervous about her surgery and went through some mental gymnastics in the previous twenty-four hours to convince herself that spending the night at the hospital was a positive thing. Now she doesn't know what to think.

16. Teamwork.

Teamwork of a healthcare team is highly associated to a better patient experience, according to Cutler et al. in their 2019 article "Are interprofessional healthcare teams meeting patient expectations? An exploration of the perceptions of patients and informal caregivers,"[28] which was published in the *Journal of Interprofessional Care*. Their study concluded that "poor teamwork skills in healthcare have been found to be a contributing cause of negative incidents in patient care, whilst effective teamwork has been linked to more positive patient outcomes." We talked a lot in the last chapter about how to build a Contagious Camaraderie Culture. Showing that you are working as a team and that all hands are on deck to solve the customer's problem is likely to boost Client Karma.

Daniel Blum of Sinai Hospital shared a great example of how his staff worked as a team to help a patient who, for a variety of reasons, had nobody to take care of her dog while she was in the hospital. With the support of Sinai leadership, staff worked together to make sure the dog was fed and safe while the patient recovered.

17. An Aesthetically Appealing Physical Space.

Let's start with the basics. Patients, clients, and their family caregivers are obviously going to be put off by dirty, unkempt healthcare institutions. In their 2020 article, "A Qualitative Analysis of Patient, Provider, and Administrative Perceptions and Expectations About Patients' Hospital Stays,"[29] published in the *Journal of Patient Experience*, Nepal et al. highlighted that the cleanliness of an institution is very important to patients. Rick Evans at NewYork-Presbyterian Hospital agrees. He said that this became even more important to patients during the pandemic.

Not only is a dirty institution just plain gross, many laypeople are very aware of the possibility of a hospital acquired infection (HAI) when entering a healthcare institution. It's common sense, but keeping your physical space as clean as possible is very reassuring to patients, clients, and family caregivers. Obviously, bathrooms, patient or resident rooms, examination spaces, and equipment should be cleaned regularly. But it's important to not overlook administrative areas as well. If you are a C-suite executive, is your desk a mess? If you are private practice owner, does your receptionist have a ton of clutter in her workspace? Tidiness of a workspace is very reassuring to stressed patients, clients, and family caregivers. If there's an administrator who doesn't see patients and just can't keep their office organized, at least get that employee to keep their door shut if patients and clients are walking by!

18. If There's a Choice, Be Sure to Ask Their Preference.

Personally, I think expecting someone to share a hospital, nursing home, or assisted living room is cruel. I can't even imagine having to share a room with anyone other than my husband. Well, maybe with a close girlfriend or a family member—but only for a night or two. Residents at nursing homes and sometimes even at assisted living communities share rooms every day, as do hospital and rehab patients. I can't imagine being put in a room with a stranger when I feel my absolute worst, when I haven't showered for a couple days, while I'm on mind-numbing drugs, or while only a thin curtain protects my privacy. But that's me. I would have assumed all people would feel that way. Turns out, the data is mixed.

Roos et al. found in their 2020 study, "Trading company for privacy: A study of patients' experiences,"[30] that there were upsides of shared patient rooms. "Patients had ambiguous views on whether multiple-bed rooms or single-bed rooms were to be preferred. Main results include how patients cherished 'the importance of others' but at the same time valued "the importance of privacy." Being hospitalized in multiple-bed rooms was, for many patients, a very positive experience in terms of social interaction. Patients in single-bed rooms reported being more dependent on nurses to maintain social contact and obtain safety."

But other studies indicate that patients benefit and are more satisfied with private rooms.

In a study of one thousand patients, Blandfort et al. found that "the risk of delirium is reduced in single-bed rooms compared with multiple-bed rooms in geriatric wards." Their study, "Single-bed rooms in a geriatric ward prevent delirium in older patients,"[31] was published in *Aging Clinical and Experimental Research* in 2020.

Hosseini and Bagheri's study "Comparison of Patient Satisfaction with Single Patient Rooms Versus Shared Patient Rooms,"[32] published in 2017 in the *Annals of Military and Health Sciences Research*, found that patients were much more satisfied when they had a private room. They found that "the most important advantages of single patient rooms are improved quality of sleep, preserving patients' privacy and autonomy in order to achieve greater control over their environment, and better communication with staff and healthcare workers."

While private rooms may not be a possibility at every hospital, nursing home or other inpatient facility, I believe it's important to work toward that eventual goal in the interest of better customer service *and* better clinical outcomes. Sure, if someone prefers to share, they can be given that option. But can you imagine the difference all-private rooms would have made for nursing home, assisted living, and hospital patients during the pandemic?

Speaking of personal preferences, a fascinating study, "Exploring the Relationship between Window View Quantity, Quality, and Ratings of Care in the Hospital,"[33] discussed the impact of windows in hospital rooms. Mihandoust et al. explored 650 hospital patients' opinion on windows in the 2021 study published in *International Journal of Environmental Research and Public Health.*

"Windows in the patient rooms impact the key patient satisfaction measures and patient experience during the hospital stay. Patient room design, bed set up, and quantity and quality of window views may play an important role in shaping the patient's experience."

"On a scale of 0–10—participants with access to windows gave a 1-unit higher rating for the hospital. Access to window views from their bed provided a 1-unit increase and having a view to green spaces resulted in a 2-unit increase in hospital ratings," they found.

I'm guessing this makes a lot of sense to you; it makes a lot of sense to me. I love natural light. I once made the mistake of living in a home that didn't have much natural light, and I was shocked how negatively it impacted my mood. But I think it would be a mistake to assume that everyone would prefer a room with a window. Some individuals—particularly those housed on a first floor—might even feel more vulnerable if they'd ever been the victim of a crime and had the concern that somebody could break into their room. While often we don't have options to offer a patient, client, or resident, we should make it a practice to ask when we do.

Another great example of honoring preference is something that Home Instead Senior Care is in the process of rolling out in partnership with their new owner, Honor Technology. Chad Brough, vice president of healthcare transformation, says their system will pair their professional CARE Pros with the most compatible clients. For example, let's say there's a client who will be very disappointed if their CARE Pro doesn't show up for their four-hour shift at exactly 2:00 p.m. on the dot. That client would be paired up with a CARE Pro who is very regimented about time. If a client is less concerned about the exact time the CARE Pro shows up, as long as she is there for the full four hours, he would be paired with a CARE Pro who might occasionally get stuck in a bit of traffic.

19. Don't talk about patients or clients like they aren't in the room.

Years ago, my middle-aged Uncle Fran had to get a kidney transplant. Miraculously, my Aunt Kathy, his wife, was a match! After he had surgery, all our family members were taking turns visiting with him. While I was visiting, Uncle Fran was sitting up in bed in his hospital gown, and we were watching basketball—his favorite—on television. When a doctor came to the room, Uncle Fran turned down the volume of the basketball game so he could hear what the doctor had to say. Disappointingly, the doctor barely acknowledged him while addressing all of his comments and questions to *me!* I smirked and said, "You know, he's right there." The doctor then began redirecting his comments and eye contact toward Uncle Fran.

I have seen that scenario play out countless times over the course of my career in health, mental health, and senior living. It's most obvious when the patient or client is elderly or a child. But everyone is vulnerable to this treatment when they "look like a patient." In Uncle Fran's case, that meant sitting in a hospital bed and wearing a hospital gown. For other people, it could be that they are using a wheelchair, walker, cane, or hearing device. For others, it's simply the nature of their diagnosis: the staff person chooses not to engage with them directly because they have Alzheimer's disease, schizophrenia, or any number of cognitive or mental health conditions.

Of course, there are times when a health or mental health provider needs to speak directly to the parent of a child or the family caregiver of a loved one. But if that conversation is taking place in front of the patient, he or she must not be ignored.

Ten-year-old Charlotte is back in the hospital because of her asthma and allergies. Dr. Wilson comes into the room and begins talking to Charlotte's parents about the course of treatment and what she's going to recommend upon discharge. Certainly, Charlotte's parents need to hear this information, because Charlotte is a minor and her parents are responsible for her care. But when Dr. Wilson refers to Charlotte as "her" and "she" in the conversation, is not making any eye contact with the child, and is acting as though she were not present, this is insensitive. If Dr. Wilson feels that she wanted to say something that is too delicate for Charlotte to hear, then she should ask the parents to step into the hallway or another room for a private conversation.

It's bad enough that this happens to children, but it probably happens even more to older adults. Particularly when an older adult has dementia, many health, mental health, and even senior living staff begin treating that person as though he or she were invisible. If someone's in the room, make sure they feel included.

20. Communicate often (especially when there's a wait).

Just recently, I went to a new doctor's office for a 10:00 a.m. appointment. There was nobody in the office besides the receptionist and me. At 10:10 a.m. I asked the receptionist how far behind the doctor was running. She looked at me blankly and said, "He's running on time." I pointed out that he was already running ten minutes late. I wasn't in a rush, but it was irritating to be told that my appointment was going to start on time when I'd already been waiting for ten minutes.

I wound up being brought back to the doctor's examination room at 10:15 a.m. And it really wasn't such a big deal—I always bring something to work on when I may be in a waiting room. But wouldn't it have been nice if, when I arrived, the receptionist greeted me with "Welcome! Please accept our apologies that the doctor is running a bit behind. He will see you in about ten to fifteen minutes." This would have let me know what to expect. If I had phone calls to return, I could have stepped outside the office. If I wanted to run into the post office next door to buy stamps, I could have gotten that done.

21. Show That You Want Their Feedback.

Surveys and questionnaires are great. They do *tell* that you are interested in hearing from your patients and clients. But they can also be time-consuming and "one more thing" that your busy patient or client needs to do. But what if you showed them that you want their feedback on-site? One great example is the display Rite Aid has in their stores. This colorful machine has four buttons: one with a very happy face, one with a decidedly unhappy face, and two in the middle that indicate "sort of happy" or "sort of unhappy." A sign above it says, "How satisfied were you with your pharmacy having your prescription ready when promised?" Even if a customer does not choose to engage with the machine, this is a clear *show* that Rite Aid is interested in feedback. Just viewing this machine may encourage a patient to find an employee to share both positive and negative comments.

22. Showing (not just telling) that you serve diverse populations.

Anton Gunn, MSW, CSP, is the former chief diversity officer at Medical University of South Carolina and a former adviser to President Barack Obama. Currently, he helps leaders and organizations become more socially conscious through keynote speeches and coaching. He advises, "Make sure that somebody on the clinical team looks like the patients that you serve." He says that members of diverse groups who are your patients and clients might believe that you are competent even if there are no staff who resemble them. But they will not feel welcome, and they will not trust you.

During our interview for this book, Gunn asked me how I would feel as a woman going to an obstetrician-gynecologist practice that was staffed entirely by men. I responded immediately that as a young teen, that had been my first experience, and it was miserable! This metaphor really illustrates the point well.

Gunn believes that while you are working to diversify your team, it's crucial to be mindful of inclusivity in your marketing materials. Who is featured in your brochures? On your website? On signage? In your advertisements? Don't make the assumption that everyone feels welcome, even if you say that all are welcome. Be sure to include photographs and images of people of different races, religions, sexual orientations, and levels of ability. For example, can your marketing collateral feature a man wearing a yarmulke, two women holding hands, persons of different races, and an individual with a seeing-eye dog? When patients, clients, and family caregivers see someone like them represented, they are more likely to feel comfortable doing business with your organization.

23. Be mindful about generational preferences.

Speaking of diversity...Most good health, mental health, and senior living leaders and clinicians strive to be as open-minded as possible about different cultures, religions, socioeconomic statuses, and other ways that their patients and clients are different in an effort to reduce barriers to care and improve services. As we discussed in the last section, many organizations have a long way to go toward becoming more inclusive, but most are working on addressing shortcomings. But one area that is still completely overlooked is awareness of generational diversity.

Here's an acronym I use a lot when speaking about generational diversity:

AGE.

- A—accept generational diversity as part of who we are.
- G—get real about your bias.
- E—expect generational commonalities

Let's first talk about who is part of each generation and how these labels came about. First, most generational categories, with the exception of Baby Boomers, were invented by sociologists and the media. Let's start with the oldest of our population: the Traditionalists. Traditionalists include anyone born prior to 1945. These folks are a combination of what's been branded the "Silent Generation" and the "GI Generation." Baby Boomers were born between 1946 and 1964.

When we get into the younger generation, dates of inclusion become looser. Generation X typically includes persons born between 1965 and 1980, but some sources give or take a few years around 1980. Millennials are usually considered those born between 1981 and 1996, while Generation Z normally means individuals born between approximately 1997 and 2010.

Let's talk more about AGE.

A. Accepting generational diversity as part of who we are. This means that even though every person is an individual, we all are part of different diverse groups. Maybe you're an African-American Protestant female. Or perhaps you are a Caucasian Jewish gay man. Your generational affiliation is another piece of what makes you *you*. Your generational viewpoint, much like your religion, race, culture, socioeconomic status, and sexual orientation, influences the way you think, communicate, and how you make healthcare decisions.

G. Get real about your bias. This means that we all have pre-existing notions about other generations, and we should acknowledge that. Some are based on our experiences, what we've read, or even just assumptions that we make. I can't tell you how many times I've heard people assume that all their older adult patients will be "cranky." Having spent much of my career working with and writing about Traditionalists, I can tell you that is definitely not true of all older adults. But I have encountered many smart, educated people who genuinely believe that. I have also encountered many smart, educated individuals who truly believe that Millennials are the enemy because all of them are spoiled and entitled. Also not true. My cousin Sarah (the one you heard about previously who fell off the boat) is a great example of someone who defies that stereotype.

Not only did Sarah work a full-time job at a retail store while she went to college, she carried her own medical benefits. While pulling honors-level grades and holding down that job, she also became a Certified Yoga Teacher. Another example is my colleague Graeg Keogh, who works for Erickson Senior Living (where interviewee Kevin Goedecke also works) and is a Millennial. She put herself through college with a full-time job serving as a nanny to twin girls!

E. Expect generational commonalities. Expecting generational commonalities means that while all people are unique individuals, it's important to recognize the way the time in history they were born shapes them. While we don't want to make sweeping generalizations or assumptions, understanding a little bit about a person's generation helps us provide better patient-centered services to them. When we have an understanding of generational commonalities, we are better equipped to make adjustments, so our health, mental health, and senior living organizations are welcoming to all generations.

What are the commonalities of the Traditionalist generation? The oldest old of our population, these individuals tend to be the most formal, most trusting of the government, patriotic, and identify as part of an organized religion.

This generation also has the lowest levels of education. Of course, this does not mean that *every* person born 1945 or earlier has all of these traits. For example, my husband's four grandparents (all born in the 1910s) were all college graduates. They would be considered outliers.

And I'm sure everyone reading this is extremely aware of how deferent this generation is to the doctor. It's almost like the doctor can do no wrong. The family wants the patient to hire home care or stop driving? Get the doctor to say it, because that will probably incent them to make the change. In my vast experience with older adults, I have found that it's not just the doctor that's revered but anyone with an advanced education. I believe those attitudes were shaped by the fact that a good number of people in this generation didn't graduate from high school let alone have access to college.

Most people in this generation built their lives close to where they grew up and were mostly comfortable with people like them. Women working outside the home was unusual, and divorce was quite rare while these folks were growing up. These folks are typically less comfortable with people different from them simply because they were not socialized around persons of other races, economic groups, and cultures. Persons of this generation who identify as LGBT grew up being told that diverse sexual orientation required a mental health diagnosis; this is likely the most closeted generation.

Traditionalists are also typically very impressed with staff longevity in the healthcare setting, probably because changing jobs was rare for them. When they took a job, they often worked that job for the rest of their lives.

Baby Boomers shifted radically from many of their parents', grandparents', and great-grandparents' norms. This generation fought for racial and gender equality. They got divorced. Many more women in this generation were part of the workforce.

One way the Baby Boomers tend to emulate their parents, grandparents, and great-grandparents is their respect for staff longevity. They like to hear that their doctor has practiced at the hospital for the past eighteen years. They feel comforted when they know that the nurse has been with their doctor's office since she left nursing school. On the other hand, they differ from the Traditionalists, as they don't seem to have the same reverence for the doctor. Persons hailing from the Baby Boomer generation tend to view their physician as more of a partner. They are more likely to seek second opinions and do their own research than Traditionalists.

Both Baby Boomers and Traditionalists tend to look favorably on "face time." And by "face time" I am not talking about video chatting on your phone. They tend to be very impressed when they see you working on-site. Even in this post-pandemic world where working from home has become the norm, many from these generations still tend to subscribe to the belief that most real work gets done in the workplace.

Maria, a seasoned nursing director at a senior living community, specifically made her hours noon to eight three days a week. Why? Because she learned early on in her career that while she could very efficiently get her job done during the hours of nine to five, the perception of some of her residents' family members was that she was "never there" because they didn't see her during their evening visits. Many Traditionalist spouses of residents and Baby Boomer adult children assumed that if they didn't personally see her working, she must be goofing off.

Maria's strategy placated family members whose mindset valued "face time." She found that this reduced complaints and after-hours calls to her cell phone (in the early years, a pager!). Maria's strategy wouldn't work for everyone, but if your organization serves many Baby Boomers and Traditionalists who find "face time" with leaders comforting, maybe leadership can take turns being there on off-hours.

Want to build rapport with a Traditionalist or a Baby Boomer? Emphasize your longtime team members. Highlight that your organization has been serving clients for forty years. But we will learn shortly that this should not be necessarily emphasized with members of other generations.

Generation X has been nicknamed the "MTV Generation" and the "Latchkey Generation." Another common label for Gen Xers is "slacker," which I, as a Gen Xer, certainly take issue with! Gen Xers are really the first generation with large numbers of divorced parents. Their parents and grandparents are Baby Boomers, and they have emulated some of their traits but not all.

The Millennial generation has been heavily criticized by pretty much everyone. While Generation Z is considered to be the digital natives, most Millennials don't remember a time before computers and the internet either. They are extremely comfortable with diversity; in fact, they are likely to think something is wrong with your organization if it is too homogeneous. If you are expecting them to call your office for an appointment, they may do it, but they are certainly not going to like it. They are going to prefer an option to schedule an appointment virtually.

While the Traditionalists and Baby Boomers are delighted to see your staff working a lot, Millennials and Generation Zers are usually going to be concerned when they see that. Most Millennials and Generation Zers care about a work-life balance. If they see the administrator or director of nursing at their mother's or grandmother's senior living community there at all hours, they often wonder why those staff are so inefficient. Or worse, the younger generations may be wondering if those staff are burned out and question if that community is the right place for their loved ones.

They also are less likely to be impressed with staff longevity. Or more specifically, a staff person who has been in the *same position* for a long time. They're probably thinking, *Aren't they bored? Are they stagnating? Can't they move up the ladder? I guess another company wouldn't hire them....*

So what *does* impress Millennial and Generation Z patients, clients, and family caregivers? They want to see diversity reflected in both your staff and clientele. They care about your socially conscious initiatives. Sharing that your staff does a volunteer day at an animal shelter, that they build houses for Habitat for Humanity, or that your organization has a team for the American Heart Association's Heart Walk would be of interest to them. They are also going to be very concerned if they can't find out anything about you online. Digital presences are important to most healthcare customers, but to Millennials and Generation Zers, they are absolutely essential.

Most people from most generations (except possibly Traditionalists) are probably going to look you and your organization up online. But Millennials and Generation Zers are most likely to be concerned when your digital footprint is lacking. If your website is old, your blogs haven't been updated for years, or if your organization doesn't have social media accounts, there will be concern. And if you have no online presence whatsoever? That will be a red flag for the younger generations. This signals that you are out of touch and not keeping up with the times. While this chapter is about transforming patients, clients, and family caregivers from "hateful" to "grateful," it's worth noting that prospective employees from the younger generations will be reassured by a strong, clear, up-to-date online presence.

Alan Levin of NewYork-Presbyterian Queens says, "I talk up social media at new hire orientation." His robust staff recognition program that we talked about in the last chapter includes lots of social media. He hopes that prospective and current team members "think it's cool that your CNO is on Instagram." This likely contributes to Team Karma, which of course begets Client Karma.

What specifically does accommodating generational preferences mean? Let's take a look at some examples from outside of healthcare. I'm a Gen Xer. When I go to the airport, I don't want to waste time interacting with staff. I want to head to the nearest coffee shop and get to work on my laptop or, when heading out on vacation, head to an airport bar for a cocktail! My preference is to check in for my flight before I get there and download the boarding pass on my phone. But my mother-in-law, Ann, who is a Traditionalist? She doesn't have a smartphone, and she doesn't want one. When she gets to the airport, she can choose to either print her boarding pass at a kiosk or interact with an airline employee. Airlines do a great job of offering a variety of options for checking in to a flight that are generationally sensitive.

Of course, just because Traditionalists have the lowest rates of smartphone ownership doesn't mean there aren't smartphone enthusiasts in this age group. In fact, one of my favorite examples of someone who seems to be extremely tech-savvy is actor and activist George Takei, perhaps known best for his role on *Star Trek*. Takei is in his eighties and is extremely active on social media, boasting nearly ten million followers on Facebook and over three million followers on Twitter. So of course, some Traditionalists check in to their flights the way I do. But it's wonderful that we have many options.

Fast-food and fast-casual food establishments have also done a great job accommodating generational preferences. You can still walk into (or drive through in some cases) McDonald's, Panera, Chipotle, and Chick-fil-A and order your meal the old-fashioned way. But many of these restaurants also have kiosks where you can place your order, avoiding interacting with their staff. Also, you can order your food on an app for pickup. And you can even have their products delivered to your home in most geographic locations using DoorDash, Uber Eats, or other apps!

Fast-casual restaurants and fast-food establishments are accommodating customers of all age groups. How well are you doing with this?

Some health, mental health, and senior living organizations are very proud of the fact that they've gone paperless. Not only is it easier for their patients and clients, it's good for the environment, they proudly proclaim. But it's not easier for every patient and client. Maybe your practice asks new patients to complete paperwork ahead of time, before their first appointment. You direct them to your website. This is going to be very off-putting to some patients—particularly many Traditionalists and even some Baby Boomers. Do you still have an option for mailing the forms to their home if that is what they'd prefer?

Many healthcare organizations utilize MyChart or a similar system for scheduling appointments, getting blood work results, and requesting prescription refills. While many people love this, some do not have a computer or smartphone at home, and they are usually Traditionalists. In order to provide great service to the Traditionalists and any other patients who don't want to access technology, it's important to allow them to call your offices. It's also not unreasonable for these patients to request instructions, blood work results, and their medical charts by mail. But it's practical for healthcare organizations to consider charging modest fees for those services that require office staff's time.

On the other hand, some health, mental health, and senior living organizations are still acting like it's the Stone Age. Even if they are already a longtime patient or client, there's no way for them to schedule their next appointment without calling your office. Many members of Generation Z and Millennials will put off calling because they hate picking up the phone, or might even go as far as to find another provider.

I know a lot of senior living, nursing home, and home care providers who have shifted all of their marketing and communication to online only. They advertise their marketing events and open houses on Facebook, LinkedIn, Instagram, and Twitter. They do e-blasts to their databases. They have put all of their budget into digital. This is a huge mistake. Yes, a lot of their marketing is focused on reaching adult children of elderly persons. Many Baby Boomers and pretty much all Millennials and Gen Xers spend a lot of time on their computers and smartphones. But what about the Traditionalist spouse who is taking care of her husband and could use your service? Is your marketing and communication missing her entirely?

Marketing to and communicating with Traditionalists and even some Baby Boomers benefits from some of the more old-fashioned methods. Senior living, home health, and nursing home industries who still send event invitations to prospects via the US Postal Service have an advantage over those who rely solely on digital marketing. Those who advertise their services and programs in newspapers and magazines are going to have an advantage over those who do not. Traditionalists, in particular, still like to get newsprint on their hands.

That said, just as you can't assume every Catholic goes to Mass every Sunday, or that every Latino family follows the patriarchal system, not every person of a specific generation follows its norms.

Just as it's important to be sensitive to the ways our patients, clients, and family caregivers of different generations like to receive information and access services, it's also best practice to be mindful about how our clinicians and staff individually converse with those who hail from a different generation.

It's always a good idea to consider if a comment or remark puts space between the patient and the staff person or if it bonds them. We tend to get a lot of training on this as it relates to other areas of diversity but not so much when it comes to age.

Ava is seventy-five-year-old, and she is seeing Dr. Oliver, a thirty-five-year-old orthopedic surgeon, for a consult. When Dr. Oliver walks into the room where she is waiting, Ava tells him he looks just like a younger William Hurt. Dr. Oliver frowns and says he doesn't know who that is. Ava smiles and says, "Oh, sure you do. He's been in so many good movies. *The Big Chill, Children of a Lesser God...*Oh, you definitely know him; he was also on that show *Damages* for a while." Dr. Oliver responds, "No, idea. I guess that was before my time. Anyway, let's talk about why you are here...."

Was there a way that Dr. Oliver could've responded without making Ava feel like she was an ancient old lady on his to-do list for the day? What if Dr. Oliver said, "I'm not sure who that is. I will have to google him later." Or better yet, in an effort to build rapport, he could have said, "I don't know William Hurt's work, but let me google a picture of him right now. I've got to see this guy who looks so much like me!"

Either response would've taken a less than a minute, and it would've bonded the clinician and the patient rather than put generational space between them. And Ava probably would've walked out of there saying what a nice guy Dr. Oliver was rather than feeling that she was out of touch.

This generational distancing happens in the other direction in health, mental health, and senior living all the time too.

Fifteen-year-old Natalie has been seeing her twenty-eight-year-old psychologist Dr. Davidson for several years because of an anxiety disorder. During last week's session, she tells Dr. Davidson that she has begun seeing a sixteen-year-old boy from her high school. She declares that she's in love. Dr. Davidson smiles and rolls his eyes, saying, "Natalie, you are way too young to know that you are in love."

In this case, not only is Dr. Davidson putting generational distance between herself and the patient, but this is also an example of an ineffective, possibly even unethical, counseling strategy.

24. Find ways to delight when you can.

Being a patient or client is hard. Being a family caregiver is exhausting. Pleasant surprises go a long way toward building Client Karma.

John Dumas of Service Coordination and Montcordia says, "Our team is empowered to provide a hyper-personalized experience to every client and family. For example, direct care team members receive a monthly stipend that they use creatively to brighten their client's day. This might be used to surprise a client with their favorite flowers, baked goods, or anything else that will bring a smile." What can you do to emulate Dumas's strategy in your practice setting?

Building Client Karma is a process. You don't have to do this all at once. If you really need to overhaul your patient engagement and customer service practices, just start by deciding on an overall strategy. Or maybe pick one of the above suggestions to pilot. But don't assume your staff knows how to implement a strategy or suggestion without explicit instruction and training. The next chapter will help you figure out what your team needs to learn!

CHAPTER 9
Pulling It All Together: What Your Team Needs to Know How to Do

Please don't make assumptions that your team members understand or can practice *anything* about good bedside manner, customer service, or the patient experience. *Even if they are nice, friendly people.* Unless you have personally observed them demonstrate mastery of those skills, and your satisfaction surveys are affirming that, *you don't know.* Just as many organizations talk the talk about customer service but don't walk the walk, employees in health, mental health, and senior living settings often do the same. The bottom line is that many team members need training and regular reminders of what you expect to create Client Karma.

We talked earlier about how much I hate the expression "no problem."

And I've already said that I only hire nice, friendly people at Jenerations Health Education. Well, even though they are all nice, friendly, and professional—I have had to train my team not to say "no problem." Even when we hire the nicest, most professional, educated, intelligent team members, we cannot expect them to read our minds and understand the standards of our organization without proper training and coaching.

That said, we can expect reluctance to accepting training in this area. In *Communication the Cleveland Clinic Way*, Dr. Adrienne Boissy and Dr. Tim Gilligan discuss how the Cleveland Clinic created a communications improvement program for their physicians, medical students, and other "higher-level" clinicians. They met quite a bit of resistance to their training program and were surprised about it. Seasoned physicians didn't believe they needed it or thought it was a waste of time. Medical students reported that "they studied communication skills in medical school, and then the skills were effectively squashed out during training."

Let's take a step out of healthcare for a moment and talk about academia. My company, Jenerations Health Education Inc., has been a placement site for both graduate and undergraduate student interns over the last several years. Our internships are highly desirable to many students because we offer a virtual option. But it still boggles my mind how many students interviewing for a job essential to their ability to graduate show up not demonstrating basic professional readiness skills. During these interviews I have observed students appear on Zoom:

- late or not at all (without notifying us)
- dressed in clothes intended for a trip to the gym
- with their hair uncombed
- not having any idea what our organization does
- not having read the internship job description
- having pets and children running around in the background
- at a public place where there's lots of background noise

- telling me their personal problems and stressors when I start off the interview by saying, "Nice to meet you. How are you today?"

Some students send resumes and emails with lots of typos. Still others don't respond to our attempts to schedule the interview. Sadly, these gaffes have occurred not just with traditional-age students (seventeen to twenty-three) but also with returning, more mature students who have had plenty of life and work experience. I only mention that because I have much more patience with gaffes when they come from someone who is just starting to navigate a professional environment than I do with someone who is more seasoned.

The reason I share our experience with screening interns is because almost all of these students' resumes and cover letters will boast that they are "professional," "detail-oriented," and have "excellent writing" and "outstanding interpersonal skills." These students who interview so poorly are *telling* but not *showing*, just like a lot of employees in healthcare settings.

Now, are these students intentionally sabotaging their interviews? I don't think so. I believe it's one of two issues: they have either not yet internalized professional interviewing skills or they don't care to—they are not cut out to be in a professional setting.

When I say that in some cases they haven't yet internalized professional interviewing skills, I don't mean that they have never been trained in them. They may or may not have been. But if they have already received training on how to behave in a professional interview, it hasn't sunk in yet.

The same is true of customer service, patient experience, and good bedside manner skills. If the employee is not demonstrating these skills, it's possible that he has not ever been trained on them. It's also possible he has been trained, but he needs much more reinforcement of those principles and concepts before he's able to *show* in addition to *tell*.

Some healthcare institutions have security gates and security guards managing those gates. When I arrive on-site to do a speaking engagement, often the security guard is the first person I meet. The guard will ask me where I am going, and I will tell him I'm headed to Building A for an event and that I am the speaker. I can't tell you how many times I have arrived early for a speaking engagement that hundreds of visitors are expected to attend and have the guard respond gruffly with "What event?"

The fact that the literal gatekeeper does not know that an event is taking place on the organization's campus within an hour or two is a major problem. Frankly, I don't really care how the security guard treats me; I am being paid a lot of money by the organization to do a job. While it would be more pleasant if the security guard expected me, the real customer service fail is when the audience this organization wants to impress shows up and they are not welcomed with details about where to park.

When a healthcare organization invites me to speak on-site and opens up the event to visitors, it is purely for the opportunity to build and/or enhance relationships with those guests. The visitors may be other healthcare leaders and professionals who are in a position to make referrals. The visitors may be prospective patients and their family caregivers who may be great candidates for the organization's services.

When a guest shows up for the event and is met by a security guard who doesn't even know an event is happening, what message is that sending? If you are a healthcare leader or clinician, would you want to refer your patients here? If you are a prospective patient or family caregiver, would you be eager to utilize their services?

And never mind this event. Prospective patients are thinking, *If they don't know what's going on tonight, will they know where to direct me the day I come for the surgery I'm a nervous wreck worrying about?*

So how does a leader at this healthcare institution deal with the poor customer service situation at the security gate?

Many of them would probably just suggest that the security gate supervisor have a conversation with that individual security guard. But does the security gate supervisor always know how to do the customer service coaching? If you feel confident that she does, great—that might be the answer. But what if this is a pervasive problem? What if many of the security guards are unfriendly and unaware of what's going on throughout their campus? It may be that there was insufficient training on customer service and a breakdown in communication when events are happening.

When I am brought in to do customer service presentations at healthcare organizations, I sometimes catch some leaders rolling their eyes when I talk about SHANE—smiling, saying hello, ask if the patient or client needs help, nodding your head, and making eye contact. I also talk about apologizing and the importance of positive facial expressions and body language.

"Of course, our team knows all about smiling, nodding, and facial expressions," the executives who hire me say. "How ridiculous to spend any of our valuable training time and dollars on something everyone knows how to do." Maybe they do know how to practice the principles of SHANE, but they just aren't doing it. Or maybe they know about SHANE, but they truly don't know how practice it. Or maybe they just don't know about SHANE at all. Bottom line is that almost everyone needs regular refreshers on basic customer service principles, and some of your employees genuinely need a deep-dive orientation and ongoing training.

BE CLEAR ON WHAT CREATING CLIENT KARMA MEANS TO YOUR ORGANIZATION

Leadership must be extremely clear about their expectations for customer service and patient engagement. This should be discussed extensively when a person is hired but also constantly reinforced through policy updates, town hall meetings, training, and coaching and mentoring. It is unreasonable and unfair to hold your team members to a standard that they only read about once in the organization's handbook.

Let's say this is an excerpt from your handbook:

"We have high standards for customer service. All employees will be polite and friendly to each other and to our patients, clients, and their family caregivers."

That's a great start, but it's not enough. Polite and friendly can have a different meaning for different people. It's critical to tell but also to *show* your team exactly what you are expecting.

REGULAR TRAINING WITH SIMULATIONS AND ROLE PLAY

Role playing during customer service training is not always everyone's favorite, but it is very effective for several reasons. One, it gets everyone in the room engaged in checking out how their colleagues "perform." Two, even simple role play brings to the surface how simple strategies can improve patients' perception of your service. Daniel Blum, president and CEO of Sinai Hospital, concurs. He believes in utilizing role play and simulations so team members can practice scenarios that have occurred or are likely to occur in your practice setting. But, he says, "It can't be a one-and-done kind of thing." Blum believes providing training is just part of reinforcing good customer service.

Speaking of role play, Chad Brough at Home Instead Senior Care shared a very authentic example of observing real-life role play: When founders Lori and Paul Hogan launched their company, they would interview prospective CARE Pros at their home. Paul's grandmother, Grandma Manhart, would always be in the room when the interviews were conducted. Brough says it was "sort of this unwritten test." Did the candidate acknowledge Grandma Manhart? Did they make eye contact, say hello, and include her in the conversation? After all, someone like Grandma Manhart was going to be the typical customer the CARE Pro would serve. When the candidate left, Grandma Manhart would offer feedback about how she was treated. Many candidates failed this real-life role play because they failed to develop any Client Karma with Paul's grandmother!

I was recently hired by a hospital to train their housekeeping staff on "hateful-to-grateful" principles. After going through some basics about how no hospital patient or family member is ever happy to be there, we talked about SHANE. The housekeepers and their managers had all the right answers when we talked about the positive impact of smiling, being mindful of facial expressions, and making eye contact. But fifteen minutes later, when we started role playing, they didn't seem so sure of how to implement these skills.

The role play vignette involved a housekeeper, Sadie, in the role of a patient who had just vomited and needed her floor mopped. Bob, Sadie's colleague, played the role of the housekeeper. Bob knocked on the door and Sadie said, "Come in." So far, so good. Then Bob walked in, said "Hello" with his head down and began to pretend-mop the floor. Bob didn't smile at Sadie or make eye contact. He didn't say, "I'm sorry you aren't feeling so good," or "Let me get this cleaned up for you."

It's true that customer service, good bedside manner, and patient experience skills come easier to some people than others. But most people can learn. And if they can't, they really don't belong at your organization.

At a minimum, annual in-person training with simulation and role play will help remind your team members of what skills they need to practice. Supplemented by some short videos and online courses as well as regular verbal and written reminders, this will round out the reinforcement that's needed to create and build Client Karma.

ONGOING COACHING

In a 2011 *New Yorker* magazine article,[34] Atul Gawande questioned why it's standard in so many industries to have coaches, yet it's not the norm in healthcare. Why indeed?

There are a lot of ways to do effective coaching that will build Client Karma. If you have a decent budget, and especially if you have a big customer service problem, you may want to bring in a coach like me to work on individual and group skills with team members. But you could also engage a coach like me to train peer coaches on the concepts featured in this book. Peer coaches can be selected from team members who already demonstrate a mastery of customer service skills. Someone like me would work with them on how to mentor and give constructive feedback to their peers on creating Client Karma.

Or, if you are fortunate enough to have a chief of patient experience or similar position on your team, that person may be able to create a coaching program to reinforce the principles that you have written in your policies.

DON'T FORGET TO EDUCATE ABOUT THE "ALWAYS DIFFICULT"

Even those of us who are seasoned and understand "Always Difficult" patients, clients and family caregivers find working with them to be incredibly stressful. They can test the patience of even those most adept at Client Karma. Even if we have lots of experience and training. Those less seasoned or educated about such matters, who have maybe never even heard the terms "borderline" or "phobic," will always be botching interactions with those folks. We've got to include conversations about, and strategies on, how to serve the "Always Difficult" in our training and coaching. Otherwise, expect your team members to get into power struggles when they could be de-escalating. The next chapter is all about how to manage and de-escalate clients, patients, and family caregivers who are in the "Always Difficult" category.

CHAPTER 10

Managing and De-escalating Clients and Patients Who Are "Hateful" No Matter What

This chapter will discuss how to satisfy or come close to pleasing the "Always Difficult" customer (as described in chapter 2). It will also provide strategies on how to de-escalate those who are most "hateful."

It can be discouraging. You've done everything possible to create your amazing Contagious Camaraderie Culture and build Client Karma. But you still have "Always Difficult" customers! It's important to accept that there will always be clients, patients, and family caregivers that even your most compassionate and accommodating staff just plain don't like or enjoy working with.

In chapter 2, we discussed that there are patients, clients, and family caregivers who fall into the "Always Difficult" category. Most of the time, there's a very good reason for this: substance abuse problems, untreated bipolar disorder, schizophrenia, anxiety disorders, or depression. But one of the more common (though less recognized) reasons is the presence of certain personality disorders.

Although we went through lots of strategies in chapter 8 that are likely to de-escalate, prevent problems, and satisfy customers—even the "Always Difficult"—I wanted to give you some extra tips for these especially challenging folks.

ACKNOWLEDGE THIS PERSON IS PROBABLY SUFFERING

People who have substance abuse problems or mental health conditions, including personality disorders, are usually suffering in some big ways. The "Always Difficult" patient's suffering goes beyond any physical symptoms they are dealing with, like arthritic pain. The "Always Difficult" family caregiver's suffering extends past just dealing with the stress of a husband who had a stroke. If they truly have an untreated substance abuse or mental health problem beyond that, they may have little social support and few meaningful relationships. Many of them feel bad about themselves on a regular basis. Some of them may have tried and failed to get help for the problem that is causing their "Always Difficult" behaviors. This is not an excuse for poor behavior on their part, but if you can develop some understanding and empathy, you may find it easier to work with them.

BE PROACTIVE

Kevin Goedeke of Erickson Senior Living thinks that their proactive approach helps minimize stressful situations with residents and family members who fall into this category. He believes in the 80/20 rule: 20 percent of your residents are going to take up 80 percent of your time. "That might mean you are visiting that resident on a daily basis." And it also could mean that you need to call a resident's family member every single day. It's crucial to brainstorm as a team to determine what is missing and what that resident or family really needs or wants. He shared the example of a resident who almost always wore his hearing aid...except when his daughter visited. A Murphy's Law type of situation for sure! And I'm sure all readers have experienced some version of this. In this case, Goedeke's approach was to call the daughter regularly to update her on whether or not her father was using his hearing aid.

ACTIVE LISTENING

I was especially interested in what Dr. Allan Anderson of Banner Institute had to say about this since he's been practicing psychiatry for nearly forty years and has treated plenty of individuals with personality disorder traits. Dr. Anderson recommends active listening as a preventive strategy. Even though a lot of health, mental health, and senior living professionals will say they don't have time for active listening, investing a little time now will pay dividends later. "You look for the hook," he says. When you take the time to listen, take a deep breath when someone is being difficult, and hold back from responding too soon, you will find a hook about what the "Always Difficult" person's deeper needs are. "If you can do that, you're going to win every time," he says.

Dr. Anderson prides himself on the fact that comments and feedback from patients and families at Banner routinely state outright that "the doctor listened to me." Even when serving people who have borderline traits, if they get the impression that the healthcare provider really cares, you will make progress in preventing difficult behavior. We need to expect that people who have personality disorders or strong personality traits will "try to test you." Don't defend when they have a complaint. Listen, listen, listen. Look for the hook that is "their suffering." Dr. Anderson says about staff that "people want to get defensive," and that is "exactly the wrong way to go." It's so important for staff to remember that "this is not necessarily a personal attack; it's the impressions this person has that are distorted... that causes the person to be angry, and they're venting that on me. And I can accept that. Even though it can be hard, try to have a sticks-and-stones approach when working with these folks," he says.

MANAGE YOUR SCHEDULE WHERE YOU CAN

Is your most energetic and productive time of the day morning, after lunch, evening? Can you try to work with those "Always Difficult" customers when you have the most energy? Can you try to limit how many "Always Difficult" people you are serving on a given day? While not everyone can control when they encounter an "Always Difficult" individual, some leaders' jobs will allow them to do this. If you can, try to space out the challenging interactions and have them when you know you'll be well rested and most effective.

LOOK BEYOND THE "ALWAYS DIFFICULT" BEHAVIOR

Leslie Ray, regional director of operations at LCB Senior Living, recalls many years ago when her team was trying to manage a relentlessly difficult older resident when she worked at a different company. This individual was constantly calling anyone and everyone at her community with minor complaints. Leslie challenged her team to be detectives: could they find a reason behind her constant laments? Ultimately, her team discovered this individual was very lonely. Giving her extra attention was the answer to reducing the complaints.

MAKE THE PERSON FEEL IMPORTANT

Look, all of us in health, mental health, and senior living should be striving to make our clients, patients, and their family caregivers feel as important as possible. Leslie Ray says that making a difficult person feel extra special is the key to managing narcissistic behavior. She shared the example of a staff person surprising a resident who loves cranberry juice with an extra-large glass. Ray suggests that the impact is even more profound when the staff person specifically points out, "I know how much you love cranberry juice, so I wanted to make sure you got a huge glass today." People with narcissistic traits feel entitled, and when we cater to them in this way, they typically respond very positively.

HANDLE THE SITUATION EARLY...AND AS A TEAM

Alan Levin, whom we heard from in chapter 6, has a lot of experience in helping his leaders and clinicians handle patients who are seemingly "Always Difficult." He finds that it's crucial to call a huddle—early! "We're successful with the challenging patient or family...when we have a team meeting right away." When a patient or family member is "difficult," many times, staff members are all individually trying to problem-solve, and that rarely goes better than when the whole team gets on the same page about what can be done to attempt to satisfy the patient or family.

John Dumas of Service Coordination and Montcordia concurs. "We have low supervision ratios so experienced managers are available to help families and team members navigate difficult situations and provide individualized support."

Working as a team in managing someone who is "Always Difficult" is essential, but it's crucial to avoid different team members trying to solve the same problem separately. Make sure you do a "huddle" like Levin suggests!

SET BOUNDARIES EARLY AND OFTEN

We talked about boundaries a lot in chapter 7. But they are the most important when you are working with someone who is "Always Difficult." You need to be clear about what is and is not acceptable. A patient driving to your home and knocking on your door at 8:00 p.m. because they can't get an answer to a question is absolutely not okay. Cursing at your staff is not acceptable. If you only work during the week and your organization does not provide weekend services, let clients know that they should seek medical attention from the emergency room if needed. Dual relationships can lead to particularly bad outcomes when they occur with "Always Difficult" persons. Be sure to discuss boundaries early and often with your team and communicate them early and often to your clients, patients, and family caregivers.

REWARDING BEHAVIOR YOU WANT

No, I'm not joking. It probably sounds ridiculous to talk about rewarding adults for good behavior. But again, I'm a former shrink, and I am a big believer in positive reinforcement.

If you are dealing with an "Always Difficult" individual who has borderline traits and they don't threaten to sue you when something goes wrong, be sure to thank them. Say something like, "I am grateful that you are being so gracious while having to wait." I know it sounds nuts, but a lot of times this is going to work wonders.

PROVIDE SPECIFIC TRAINING ON HOW TO DEAL WITH "ALWAYS DIFFICULT" CUSTOMERS

Dr. Kathryn Fiddler is the vice president of population at TidalHealth, a large Maryland medical system that includes hospitals and physician practices. During my interview with her, she said that mental health first-aid courses have been particularly helpful for their security team. This is available for all their staff, but Dr. Fiddler finds that this helps quite a bit with de-escalation techniques when a patient is particularly difficult.

PROMOTE SELF-CARE

We talked a lot about burnout, compassion fatigue, and countertransference in chapter 7. When someone is experiencing any or all of these issues, the odds that they are going to handle an "Always Difficult" person poorly are high. Leadership needs to be looking at who needs breaks, especially when a team member has had a lot of interactions with someone who is "Always Difficult." Empower your team members to look out for each other too, and to offer "time outs" to their colleagues who could use a few moments, a few hours, or a few days to refresh.

DON'T TAKE ABUSE

Occasionally I will get a call from an organization who says they have some "Always Difficult" patients, clients, and family caregivers and they want me to come in to train their team. When they describe the problem, I tell them that they don't need me; they need to call the police!

Physical abuse or threats should never be tolerated and should always be dealt with properly with the authorities (you should to talk to your attorney about how to manage HIPAA and confidentiality in these cases). But there are times when you have done absolutely everything you can to de-escalate, and you and your staff are being abused.

Yes, we need to have thick skin while working with "Always Difficult" people. But ongoing name-calling, insults, and cursing should not be tolerated. In addition to having written policies on what you want for Client Karma and Team Karma, you need written policies on when a customer needs to be "fired" too.

It's one thing to deal with a complainer or somebody who is always threatening to "have your license." It's another entirely when your staff are afraid for their physical safety or are being subjected to psychological abuse regularly. You frequently have the right to terminate treatment of "Always Difficult" patients, clients, and family caregivers in these cases. You just need to make sure you do it ethically and legally, according to your state regulations.

CHAPTER 11
Creating a Better Experience for Clients and Patients in Your Specific Practice Setting

While we've covered customer service best practices ideas that you can apply in any practice setting, this chapter will offer specific observations and tips for how your specific type of organization can create a less "hateful" and more "grateful" environment. Some of these suggestions will involve a modest financial investment while others require no money to implement.

CONTINUING CARE RETIREMENT COMMUNITIES (CCRC) OR LIFE CARE COMMUNITIES

Better, larger signage (modest financial investment)

Life care communities are typically huge properties that house thousands of older adults. Many of their employees will compare them to small towns. Having signs that are large enough for visually impaired residents and visitors is essential. This may seem obvious but is often missing from these communities.

SENIOR LIVING COMMUNITIES AND NURSING HOMES

Make it simple for your guests (modest financial investment)

Assisted living communities host lots of open-to-the-public events: conferences featuring guest speakers presenting about dementia, elder law, or financial planning; caregiver support groups; networking meetings; happy hours; and many others. When you are hosting any type of event open to the public, make sure it is extremely clear where your guests should park and what entrance they should use. Since the audience for these events is typically prospective residents and their families as well as professionals who can make referrals, you want to make the best possible impression. When someone spends ten minutes walking around to different entrances of your building, they are not in the best frame of mind to evaluate your community. Simply hanging some balloons or a sign is easy and will make navigating your building much easier for your guests.

Empower your residents to really make it their home (free)

In *Disrupting the Status Quo of Senior Living*, Jill Vitale-Aussem recommends moving away from rendering residents "helpless consumers." She suggests that the senior living community doesn't necessarily have to come up with all the answers for everything. Empowering the residents to take ownership of their experience in the community, in *partnership* with the staff, leads to increased satisfaction.

For example, Vitale-Aussem discusses complaints about a resident's dog which led to a resident-managed pet committee. She points to Jayne Keller's "Keeper's Committee" as another way for residents to contribute. Jayne Keller, chief operating officer at Christian Living Communities, spearheaded an initiative that involved residents coming up with ideas on how to retain staff.

Another great example is a resident garden club. It improves the aesthetics of your community, and the residents can collaborate with dining services on deciding what type of vegetables and fruits should be grown.

DENTAL OFFICES

Tell patients what to expect (free)

I never understood why so many people were phobic about going to the dentist...until about a decade ago. Having had only one tiny cavity in my entire life, I thought going to the dentist was no big deal. But when that cavity did appear, I had absolutely no idea what was next. I quickly discovered that I didn't like the sounds of the drilling, and I didn't like the sensations. But more than that, I was disappointed that nobody had told me what to expect since they knew I'd never had a filling.

Suggest ways for the patients to distract themselves (free)

I never thought much more about that dentist visit until I developed tooth sensitivity a few years later. This development led me to dread the dentist even more because I continued to be uncomfortable with the sounds and sensations. In an effort to manage my discomfort, I eventually asked the dental hygienist if I could listen to my headphones. She looked at me dumbfounded and said, "Of course." Well, it had never occurred to me to try to distract myself in this way, but it was clear to me from her reaction that lots of other patients listened to music and podcasts to distract themselves from cleanings and other dental procedures.

Why hadn't anyone suggested this to me? I had been dreading going to the dentist for years. Now when I have an appointment, I plan what fun podcast I'm going to listen to, and I look forward to the appointment...almost.

Do a better job with privacy (free)

Most dental studios have an open floor plan with cubicles dividing patients. Everyone can hear everything! If you need to review medical history, medications, or any private, sensitive information, please take that patient to a private area where you can have a conversation.

PHARMACIES

Improve privacy (free)

Retail pharmacies (and grocery stores/big-box stores with pharmacies) are a unique healthcare setting, primarily because they aren't exclusively healthcare settings. Yes, they fill prescriptions and provide vaccinations. Some retail pharmacies even offer urgent care and laboratory testing too. But beyond those clear medical services, they also sell lots of other items. Traditional retail pharmacies, like CVS, Rite Aid, and Walgreens, and the local privately owned smaller companies carry greeting cards, magazines, toiletries, makeup, laundry detergent, and food products. Grocery stores with pharmacies inside, like Giant, Wegmans, Publix, Stop & Shop, and Safeway, often also house bakeries, delis, Starbucks, and an enormous selection of food and other household necessities. Big-box stores like Target and Walmart have onsite pharmacies alongside snack bars, gardening items, furniture, food, and other sundries.

Since their employees can often be found ringing up gum, mulch, milk, diapers, and mascara along with prescriptions, it's no wonder there are constant privacy breaches at retail pharmacies.

As we discussed in chapter 8, disregard for confidentiality is a big way we can transform patients and clients from "hateful" to "more hateful." Nobody really wants to need a prescription, a shot, lab work, or an appointment at the urgent care center at your pharmacy. They want it even less when they feel you don't take their privacy seriously.

I was in a retail pharmacy in our small town after receiving a flu shot and waiting for my husband to finish receiving his. As I browsed the makeup aisle, I overheard three different phone calls the pharmacy technicians had with patients. Specific patient names and details about their medications were loudly discussed. After the third call, I found the pharmacist and let him know what had happened. He profusely apologized and said that because the pharmacy was so busy that day, his team was making phone calls by the cash register rather than in the back room. He promised to remedy the situation.

Kudos to this pharmacist for owning up to the mistake, apologizing, and turning it around. While there was a confidentiality breach, it was definitely a "hateful-to-grateful" experience for me. But what about those patients whose private medical information was shared with anyone waiting or browsing near the pharmacy counter? Since this pharmacy is located in a small town, it is very possible that *someone* who knew these individuals overheard the calls. But regardless of whether it is a small town or big city, it's really unacceptable for anyone else to hear private medical information without the explicit consent of the patient. Make sure your staff are very careful about using patient names and names of drugs in public areas.

DOCTOR'S OFFICES, PSYCHOTHERAPY OFFICES, ANY OTHER PRACTICE SETTING THAT HAS A WAITING ROOM

There are a lot of easy, cheap strategies to transform a "hateful" waiting room to a "grateful" one. Nobody likes waiting. But waiting can be more pleasant.

Have free Wi-Fi (modest financial investment)

Adults can work. Kids can play games. Everyone is quiet and less likely to complain (that is, if the devices are on silent). Speaking of which, go ahead and put up a friendly sign that says something along the lines of "Enjoy our FREE Wi-Fi (Please turn off the volume on your device)."

Do I enjoy getting my annual mammogram? No. But I am always early for all my appointments and am grateful to Advanced Radiology in Annapolis, Maryland, for the free Wi-Fi so I can get some work done while I wait.

Reading material (modest financial investment)

Have a variety of reading materials. Subscribe to at least a half dozen magazines likely to appeal to your demographic. Clear away anything older than six months.

Refreshments: (modest financial investment)

Provide a water cooler. Being even a little bit thirsty is annoying, and annoyed is not the frame of mind you want when your patient or client comes into your office. If you want to really go the extra mile, have a coffee and tea station.

HOSPITALS

Demonstrate your commitment to confidentiality (modest financial investment)

Post signs that signal your commitment to confidentiality. Not only do these reassure patients but they are essential reminders for your staff. I was recently at St. Mary Medical Center in Langhorne, Pennsylvania, and noticed a terrific wall hanging. It featured two little girls wearing old-fashioned nurse's caps and stethoscopes. They both were posing with a finger over their closed mouths. The caption said, "We respect patient confidentiality." A brilliant example of *showing* and not just *telling*.

Create a business center (modest financial investment)

Whenever my grandmother was ill, I obviously hated that she was sick, but I was very grateful to the hospital where she would be admitted. Holy Redeemer Hospital in Huntingdon Valley, Pennsylvania, shows that they care about their family caregivers. Not only do they have free Wi-Fi, they actually have a business center that is open to visitors. Desks! Computers! What a forward-thinking concept!

Have decent, healthy, food in the cafeteria (modest financial investment)

Hospitals are notorious for bad food. And that's a pity because patients need to eat well in order to regain their strength and health.

When the cafeteria at the hospital has lousy food, it sends a strong message. *What on earth is my loved one eating up in their room? How could they be getting better if the food is so bad?* When the hospital has good food in its cafeteria, it is very reassuring to family caregivers who are visiting.

And sure, a certain amount of junk food should be available in the cafeteria. When family and friends visit, they are stressed out, and a lot of times they want some comfort food. But a hospital is supposed to be a place of healing. Make sure there is a good selection of healthy meals, snacks, and beverages so frequent visitors can keep up their stamina.

MENTAL HEALTH/PSYCHOLOGICAL/COUNSELING PRACTICES

Be especially kind (free)

We discussed in chapter 8 how crucial it is to have friendly, compassionate receptionists. But this is a practice setting where it is absolutely essential. It takes an awful lot of courage for most people to call for a psychological or psychiatric appointment. The last thing they need is to encounter a rude person when they finally make that call.

ANY PRACTICE SETTING WHERE YOU ARE GOING TO GIVE A TREATMENT TO A PATIENT OR CLIENT, ESPECIALLY FOR THE FIRST TIME

Alan Levin, whose great advice we discussed earlier, said that his team at NewYork-Presbyterian Queens follows the AIDET model for offering treatment to patients. AIDET is a framework developed by consulting firm Studer Group to improve healthcare communication. Here are the basics:

Acknowledge—Greet patient or client by name

Introduce—Make sure the patient knows your name and role

Duration—Discuss how long you will be with them or when they will get the help or service they need

Explain—Let them know what will happen next and answer their questions

Thank—thank them for their time

Does your organization do any version of this? Imagine the problems that could be avoided if patients and clients were always greeted by name and they knew yours. What if they knew every time how long an appointment would last or how long an uncomfortable procedure was going to take? How would your practice reduce problems if patients and clients knew you appreciated them?

CONCLUSION

Never forget that your patients, clients, and family caregivers don't want to need you. But by acknowledging this and making a commitment to improving your customer service, you can transform them from "hateful" to "grateful."

Please reach out to me with your success stories and how you are *showing* and not just *telling*!

On social media:

- Jenerations Health Education, Inc. (facebook.com)
- Jenerations Health Education, Inc. | LinkedIn
- Jennifer L. FitzPatrick MSW CSP Jenerations Health (@fitzpatrickjen) / Twitter
- Jennifer L. FitzPatrick (@jenniferl.fitzpatrick) • Instagram photos and videos
- Jenerations Health Education, Inc. - YouTube

Or contact our office:

- contact@jenerationshealth.com
- 443-416-7710
- www.jenerationshealth.com

Thanks for reading and thanks for all you do for your patients, clients, residents, and family caregivers every day.

THANK YOU, INTERVIEWEES!

To say that these individuals are busy is an understatement. I sincerely appreciate the time these leaders took to answer my nosy questions about what works and what doesn't to better the patient, client, and family caregiver experience!

Allan Anderson, MD, MBA, is a geriatric psychiatrist, director of Banner Alzheimer's Institute at Banner Health in Tucson, Arizona, and former assistant professor of psychiatry at Johns Hopkins University in Baltimore. The former president of the American Association of Geriatric Psychiatry (AAGP), he currently serves as a delegate from the AAGP to the American Medical Association House of Delegates. Dr. Anderson earned his degrees from Virginia Tech, Carnegie Mellon University, and the University of Medicine and Dentistry of New Jersey, now the New Jersey Medical School. For more information on Banner Alzheimer's Institute at Banner Health, please check out www.banneralz.org.

Daniel Blum, MS, is the president of Sinai Hospital of Baltimore and Grace Medical Center as well as a senior vice president at LifeBridge Health. Blum has more than twenty years' experience serving as a C-suite hospital leader in both New York and Maryland. A graduate of New York University, he began his career in healthcare as a paramedic. For more information about LifeBridge Health, Sinai Hospital, and Grace Medical Center, go to www.lifebridgehealth.org.

Chad Brough, MBA, is the vice president of healthcare transformation at Nebraska-based Home Instead Senior Care. His background includes over twenty-five years of patient experience and healthcare customer service leadership in different healthcare settings. Brough earned his degrees at Indiana University Southeast and Hanover College. To find out about more about Home Instead, go to www.homeinstead.com.

Terri Cunliffe, MS, is the president and CEO of Covenant Living. Covenant Living provides hospice, in-home care, assisted living, skilled nursing, and rehabilitation services in California, Colorado, Connecticut, Florida, Illinois, Michigan, Minnesota, New Hampshire, Oklahoma, and Washington. Cunliffe earned her degrees at the University of Minnesota and Nova Southeastern University. For more information about Covenant Living, please visit www.covliving.com.

John Dumas, USMC (Ret.), MBA, is the president and chief executive officer of Washington, DC-area nonprofit Service Coordination, which includes Montcordia. Service Coordination offers case management and community services to persons with developmental disabilities. Dumas earned his degrees from Mount Saint Mary's University and the University of South Carolina. To learn more about John's work, check out www.servicecoord.org and www.montcordia.com.

Naim El-Aswad, MD, FACP, is the chief medical officer at Vital Signs Vital Skills LLC. He is the founder of the recently launched Warrior Recovery Center in Houston, which provides in-patient and outpatient treatment for veterans suffering from post-traumatic stress disorder (PTSD) and substance use disorders. The author of *Physician Burnout: An Emotionally Malignant Disease*, he is a graduate of American University of Beirut. A former emergency room physician, Dr. El-Aswad is an international speaker and expert on the areas of healthcare professional burnout and emotional intelligence. More about Dr. El-Aswad and his services can be found at www.vitalsigns-vitalskills.com.

Rick Evans is currently the senior vice president and chief experience officer for NewYork-Presbyterian Hospital. He was the very first chief experience officer appointed at the Massachusetts General Hospital and Massachusetts General Physicians Organization in Boston. A nationally recognized leader in the patient experience field, he serves as co-chair of the Patient Experience Policy Form supported by The Beryl Institute and as the public member on the American Nurses Credentialing Center's Magnet Recognition Program. He has also authored numerous articles on patient experience, including a regular column for Becker's Healthcare.

Evans holds a Master of Theology degree from Christ the King Seminary in East Aurora, NY and a bachelor's degree in philosophy from Wadhams Hall Seminary-College in Ogdensburg, NY.

Kathryn Fiddler, PhD, MBA, is the vice president of population health at TidalHealth on the Eastern Shore of Maryland, a medical system that includes hospitals and physician practices. Dr. Fiddler was educated at Salisbury University and University of Wisconsin-Eau Claire. She is also the chair of Salisbury University's College of Health and Human Services' advisory board. More information about TidalHealth may be found at www.tidalhealth.org.

Jeff Frum is the senior vice president of sales and marketing at Silverado, a provider of memory care, assisted living, and hospice services in ten states. He attended UCLA Anderson School of Management and UC Santa Barbara. For more information about Silverado, please visit www.silverado.com.

Peggy Funk, CAE, is the executive director at Hospice & Palliative Care Network of Maryland. The former associate director of the Maryland Pharmacists Association, Funk graduated from University of Maryland Global Campus. For more information about Hospice & Palliative Care Network of Maryland, please visit www.hpnmd.org.

Kevin Goedeke is the vice president of regional health operations for Erickson Senior Living and founder of NHA Stand-Up LLC. He is a graduate of University of Maryland, Baltimore County, and serves on the board of LifeSpan Network, the largest Maryland association of senior living and related providers. To subscribe to Kevin's e-list for tips about improving your healthcare leadership, go to newsletter@nhastandup.com. For more information about Erickson Senior Living, check out www.ericksonliving.com.

Heather Guerieri, RN, MSN, is the longtime chief executive officer of Compass, a large Maryland nonprofit hospice organization. She earned her master's degree at Towson University and her bachelor's degree from Salisbury University. For more information on Compass, please go to www.compassregionalhospice.org.

Anton J. Gunn, MSW, CDM, CSP, is a former advisor to President Barack Obama and former chief diversity officer at the Medical University of South Carolina Health System. He currently is the chief executive officer of 937 Strategy Group LLC and the author of *Just Lead: 44 Actions to Break Down Barriers, Boost Your Retention & Build a World-Class Culture* and *The Presidential Principles*.[35] Gunn is an international speaker, leadership consultant, and media contributor on workplace culture. He is also a former resident fellow at Harvard University's Kennedy School of Government. For more information, please visit www.antongunn.com.

Arif Kamal, MD, MBA, MHS, FACP, FAAHPM, FASCO, is the chief patient officer at the American Cancer Society and an associate consulting professor of medicine at Duke Cancer Institute. He was selected as one of the Top Influential Leaders Under 40 by the American Academy of Hospice and Palliative Medicine and received an Innovator Award from the Association of Community Cancer Centers. He has published over two hundred peer-reviewed articles in journals such as *JAMA*, *Journal of Clinical Oncology*, *Annals of Internal Medicine*, and *Lancet Oncology*. Dr. Kamal holds grant funding from the National Cancer Institute, National Institute on Aging, and Blue Cross Blue Shield of North Carolina Foundation. For more information about the American Cancer Society, please go to www.cancer.org.

George King is the director of practice operations at For All Seasons Inc., a nonprofit outpatient mental health and rape crisis center in Maryland. King's background includes more than a decade in patient experience and operations. Check out For All Seasons' website at www.forallseasonsinc.org.

James Lee, MBA, is the co-founder and CEO of Bella Groves, a San Antonio, Texas, residential and community-based support organization for persons living with dementia and their family caregivers. Lee earned his degrees from University of Texas McCombs School of Business and Texas Lutheran University. To learn more about Lee, please visit www.bellagroves.com.

Alan Levin, DNP, MBA, RN, CPHQ, NEA-BC, is the vice president and chief nursing officer at New York-Presbyterian Queens. Dr. Levin earned his degrees at University of Delaware, Seton Hall University, and Frances Payne Bolton School of Nursing at Case Western Reserve University. New York-Presbyterian Queens can be found at www.nyp.org.

Denise Manifold is the vice president of sales at Brightview Senior Living. She earned her master's degree in health promotion from the University of Delaware. Brightview has forty-eight locations and provides senior living and memory care services in Massachusetts, Connecticut, Rhode Island, New York, New Jersey, Pennsylvania, Maryland and Virginia. For more information, please go to www.brightviewseniorliving.com.

Janice Martin is the founder of Senior Liaison of Central Florida Inc. and has more than a decade of experience in healthcare and senior living. Her website is www.seniorliaisoncfl.com.

Leslie Ray is the regional director of operations at LCB Senior Living. She is also the president of LifeSpan Network and earned her degrees at University of North Carolina-

Chapel Hill and UNC Greensboro. Visit LCB's website at www.lcbseniorliving.com.

Cara Silletto, MBA, CSP, is the author of *Staying Power: Why Your Employees Leave and How to Keep Them Longer* and the founder of Magnet Culture, a company that helps organizations reduce employee turnover. She can be reached at www.magnetculture.com.

NOTES

1 Lee, Thomas. *An Epidemic of Empathy in Healthcare: How to Deliver Compassionate, Connected Patient Care That Creates a Competitive Advantage*, McGraw-Hill Education, 2016

2 "Medical error is third biggest cause of death in the US, say experts." *BMJ*, May 4, 2016; https://www.bmj.com/company/wp-content/uploads/2016/05/medical-errors.pdf

3 King, Sorrell. *Josie's Story*, Atlantic Monthly Press, 2009

4 Merlino, James. *Service Fanatics*, McGraw-Hill Education, 2014

5 Boissy, Adrienne, and Tim Gilligan. *Communication the Cleveland Clinic Way: How to Drive a Relationship-Centered Strategy for Superior Customer Service*, McGraw-Hill Education, 2016

6 Newell, Debra, and M. William Phelps. *Surviving Dirty John*, Benbella Books, 2021

7 "Ex-Tennessee nurse RaDonda Vaught sentenced to probation in patient medication death." https://www.nbcnews.com/news/us-news/ex-tennessee-nurse-radonda-vaught-sentenced-probation-patient-medicati-rcna28791

8 FitzPatrick, Jennifer L. *Cruising Through Caregiving: Reducing the Stress of Caring for Your Loved One*, Greenleaf Book Group Press, 2016

9 "The Public's Perspective on the United States Public Health System," Harvard T. H. Chan School of Public Health; https://cdn1.sph.harvard.edu/wp-content/uploads/sites/94/2021/05/RWJF-Harvard-Report_FINAL-051321.pdf

10 Platonova, Elena A., Haiyan Qu, and Jan Warren-Findlow, *Int J Health Care Qual Assur*, 2019 Mar 11;32(2):534-546. doi: 10.1108/IJHCQA-02-2018-0027; https://pubmed.ncbi.nlm.nih.gov/31017065/

11 Taylor, David McD., Rory S Wolfe, and Peter A Cameron. "Analysis of complaints lodged by patients attending Victorian hospitals, 1997–2001," *Med J Aust* 2004; 181 (1): 31-35. doi: 10.5694/j.1326-5377.2004.tb06157.x; https://www.mja.com.au/journal/2004/181/1/analysis-complaints-lodged-patients-attending-victorian-hospitals-1997-2001

12 Elias, Richard M., Karen M. Fischer, Mustaqeem A. Siddiqui, Trevor Coons, Cindy A. Meyerhofer, Holly J. Pretzman, Hope E. Greig, Sheila K. Stevens, and M. Caroline Burton. "A taxonomic review of patient complaints in adult hospital medicine," *Journal of Patient Experience* 8 (2021): 23743735211007351; https://journals.sagepub.com/doi/full/10.1177/23743735211007351

13 Kroon, Madison, and Joon Soo Park. "Negative reviews online: an exploratory analysis of patient complaints about dental services in Western Australia," *Australian Dental Journal* (2021); https://onlinelibrary.wiley.com/doi/10.1111/adj.12893 // Alamo-Palomino, Isabel J., Juan P. Matzumura-Kasano, and Hugo F. Gutiérrez-Crespo. "Patient complaints in the adult emergency department of a tertiary referral hospital," *Rev Fac Med Hum* (2020); https://www.semanticscholar.org/paper/PATIENT-COMPLAINTS-IN-THE-ADULT-EMERGENCY-OF-A-Alamo-Palomino-Matzumura-Kasano/75bfe344e10fb8e3739c54773e32c7ed7cbc5169

14 Humphrey, Kate E., Melissa Sundberg, Carly E. Milliren, Dionne A. Graham, and Christopher P. Landrigan. "Frequency and Nature of Communication and Handoff Failures in Medical Malpractice Claims," *Journal of Patient Safety* 18, no. 2 (2022): 130–137; Mammen, Oommen, James Tew, Tiffany Painter, Elizabeth Bettinelli, and Jennifer Beckjord. "Communicating suicide risk to families of chronically suicidal borderline personality disorder patients to mitigate malpractice risk," *General Hospital Psychiatry* 67 (2020): 51–57; Hanganu, Bianca, Magdalena Iorga, Iulia-Diana Muraru, and Beatrice Gabriela Ioan.

"Reasons for and facilitating factors of medical malpractice complaints. what can be done to prevent them?" *Medicina* 56, no. 6 (2020): 259

15 Appelbaum, Paul S. "Malpractice claims in psychiatry: approaches to reducing risk," *World Psychiatry*, Sept. 9, 2021; https://onlinelibrary.wiley.com/doi/10.1002/wps.20907

16 Lee, Thomas. *An Epidemic of Empathy*, McGraw-Hill Education, 2016

17 Liu, Cynthia, et al. "'But his Yelp reviews are awful!': Analysis of general surgeons' Yelp reviews," *Journal of Medical Internet Research*, April 30, 2019

18 Son, Jung Hee, Jae Hong Kim, and Gi Jin Kim. "Does employee satisfaction influence customer satisfaction? Assessing coffee shops through the service profit chain model," *International Journal of Hospitality Management* 94 (2021): 102866; Carthon, J. Margo Brooks, Linda Hatfield, Heather Brom, Mary Houton, Erin Kelly-Hellyer, Amelia Schlak, and Linda Aiken. "System-level improvements in work environments lead to lower nurse burnout and higher patient satisfaction," *Journal of nursing care quality* 36, no. 1 (2021): 7; Kang, Ji Yun, Minji K. Lee, Erin M. Fairchild, Suzanne L. Caubet, Dawn E. Peters, Gregory R. Beliles, and Linda K. Matti. "Relationships among organizational values, employee engagement, and patient satisfaction in an academic medical center," *Mayo Clinic Proceedings: Innovations, Quality & Outcomes* 4, no. 1 (2020): 8–20

19 Silletto, Cara. *Staying Power: Why Your Employees Leave and How to Keep Them Longer*, Silver Tree Publishing, 2018

20 El-Aswad, Naim. *Physician Burnout: An Emotionally Malignant Disease*, CreateSpace, 2017

21 Vitale-Aussem, Jill. *Disrupting the Status Quo of Senior Living: A Mindshift*, Health Professions Press, 2019

22 Berry, Leonard L. and Kent D. Seltman. *Management Lessons from Mayo Clinic: Inside One of the World's Most Admired Service Organizations*, McGraw-Hill Education, 2008

23 Dean, Janice. *Mostly Sunny*, HarperCollins, 2020; *Make Your Own Sunshine*, HarperCollins, 2021

24 Turner, Dee Ann. *It's My Pleasure: The Impact of Extraordinary Talent and a Compelling Culture,* Elevate, 2015

25 Avrin, David. *Why Customers Leave (and How to Win Them Back),* Career Press, 2019

26 Michelli, Joseph A. *The Starbucks Experience: 5 Principles for Turning Ordinary Into Extraordinary*, McGraw-Hill, 2006

27 ———. *The New Gold Standard: 5 Leadership Principles for Creating Legendary Customer Experience Courtesy of The Ritz-Carlton Hotel Company*, McGraw-Hill, 2008

28 Cutler, Suzanne, Charles Morecroft, Phil Carey, and Tom Kennedy. "Are interprofessional healthcare teams meeting patient expectations? An exploration of the perceptions of patients and informal caregivers," *J Interprof Care*, 2019 Jan.-Feb.;33(1):66–75

29 Nepal, Sansrita, Angela Keniston, Kimberly A. Indovina, Maria G Frank et al., "A Qualitative Analysis of Patient, Provider, and Administrative Perceptions and Expectations About Patients' Hospital Stays," *J Patient Exp.,* 2020 Dec.;7(6):1760–1770

30 Roos, Anne Karine Østbye, Eli Anne Skaug, Vigdis Abrahamsen Grøndahl, and Ann Karin Helgesen. "Trading company for privacy: A study of patients' experiences," *Nursing Ethics*, 2020 June; 27(4):1089–1102

31 Blandfort, Sif, Merete Gregersen, Kirsten Rahbek, Svend Juul, and Else Marie Damsgaard. "Single-bed rooms in a geriatric ward prevent delirium in older patients," *Aging Clinical and Experimental Research,* Aging Clin Exp Res. 2020 Jan.;32(1):141–147

32 Hosseini, Seyyed Bagher and Maliheh Bagheri. "Comparison of Patient Satisfaction with Single Patient Rooms Versus Shared Patient Rooms," *Annals of Military and Health Sciences Research*, 2017 Dec. 15(4):e80199

33 Mihandoust, Sahar, Anjali Joseph, Sara Kennedy, Piers MacNaughton, and May Woo. "Exploring the Relationship between Window View Quantity, Quality, and Ratings of Care in the Hospital," *Int J Environ Res Public Health,* 2021 Oct. 12;18(20):10677

34 Gawande, Atul. "Personal Best: Top athletes and singers have coaches. Should you?" *New Yorker*, Sept. 6, 2011; https://www.newyorker.com/magazine/2011/10/03/personal-best)

35 Gunn, Anton J. *The Presidential Principles*, Advantage Media Group, 2018

ACKNOWLEDGMENTS

Sean FitzPatrick, my amazing husband, thanks for putting up with me. Seriously. You are the best husband on the planet, and the Perfect Companion. I don't know how I got such a smart, hot, hilarious, Zen man to love me but you make me feel like the center of the world when we are together (which, let's be honest, is almost all the time).

As someone who speaks and writes professionally, I get a lot more attention than Sean does. But everyone needs to know that this incredible man in the background is my business partner, advisor, and first editor for everything I write. He makes everything I do professionally so much better.

Thank you so much to my agent, Greg Johnson, of Word Serve Literary, for believing in this book and signing me. It's been a joy to work with you.

I am grateful to Debra Englander, my editor, for your insights, advice, and of course, for acquiring this book. I'm thrilled to be part of the Post Hill Press family. Thanks also to Heather King at Post Hill for putting up with the never-ending cover debate.

Thank you to all the extremely busy executives who took the time to be interviewed for *Reimagining Customer Service in Healthcare*—you are helping make the patient/client experience a better one. I appreciate your making the time to talk with me!

I also sincerely appreciate everyone who previewed this book and provided a blurb. I promise to pay your kindness forward.

Thank you to all of my friends and family who have supported me by coming to book signings, book launches, speaking engagements, as well as sharing on social media and through word of mouth. I am fortunate to have a huge friend/family network and please know I never take you for granted.

Last, but most importantly, I thank God for all of my blessings. I am grateful every day.

ABOUT THE AUTHOR

Jennifer L. FitzPatrick, MSW, CSP is the founder of Jenerations Health Education, Inc., the author of *Cruising through Caregiving: Reducing the Stress of Caring for Your Loved One*, and an instructor at Johns Hopkins University's Certificate on Aging program. A former psychotherapist, she serves on the Care Advisory Board for Seth Rogen and Lauren Miller Rogen's nonprofit, Hilarity for Charity (HFC). A frequent media contributor, FitzPatrick's advice has been featured in *The Wall Street Journal*, *The Washington Post*, *Chicago Tribune*, *Forbes*, *Fast Company*, and on ABC, CBS, Fox News, HLN, and Sirius XM. Hailing originally from Philadelphia, she will challenge anyone to a parallel parking contest.